LIVING THE SPIRIT

Stonewall Inn Editions

Michael Denneny, General Editor

Buddies by Ethan Mordden
Joseph and the Old Man by Christopher Davis
Blackbird by Larry Duplechan
Gay Priest by Malcolm Boyd
Privates by Gene Horowitz
Taking Care of Mrs. Carroll by Paul Monette
Conversations with My Elders by Boze Hadleigh
Epidemic of Courage by Lon Nungesser
One Last Waltz by Ethan Mordden
Gay Spirit by Mark Thompson
As If After Sex by Joseph Torchia
The Mayor of Castro Street by Randy Shilts
Nocturnes for the King of Naples by Edmund White
Alienated Affections by Seymour Kleinberg
Sunday's Child by Edward Phillips
The God of Ecstasy by Arthur Evans
Valley of the Shadow by Christopher Davis
Love Alone by Paul Monette
The Boys and Their Baby by Larry Wolff
On Being Gay by Brian McNaught
Parisian Lives by Samuel M. Steward
Living the Spirit by Will Roscoe, ed.
Everybody Loves You by Ethan Mordden
Death Takes the Stage by Donald Ward
Untold Decades by Robert Patrick

LIVING THE SPIRIT

A GAY AMERICAN INDIAN ANTHOLOGY

COMPILED BY GAY AMERICAN INDIANS

WILL ROSCOE
COORDINATING EDITOR

ST. MARTIN'S PRESS
NEW YORK

The publisher would like to thank the following publishers for granting permission to reprint material herein: Grateful acknowledgment to Firebrand Books for permission to reprint three pieces from *Mohawk Trail* by Beth Brant and to the University of Nebraska Press for permission to reprint form *Lakota Belief and Ritual* by James R. Walker.

Design by ROBERT BULL DESIGN.

Library of Congress Cataloging-in-Publication Data

Living the spirit: a gay American Indian anthology / edited by Will Roscoe.
p. cm.
ISBN 0-312-01899-1
1. Homosexuality—Literary collections. 2. Gays' writings, American.
3. Lesbians' writings, American. 4. American literature—Indian authors.
5. Indians of North America—Sexual behavior—Literary collections.
6. American literature—20th century. 7. Homosexuality—United States.
8. Indians of North America—Sexual behavior. I. Roscoe, Will.
PS509.H57L58 1988 87-36691
810'.8'0353—dc19

ISBN 0-312-03475-X (Pbk.)

10 9 8 7 6 5 4 3

To our ancestors and the memory of our fallen warriors

The day I saw a poster declaring the existence of an organization of Gay American Indians, I put my face into my hands and sobbed with relief. A huge burden, the burden of isolation and of being defined only by one's enemies, left me on that enlightening day. I understood then that being Gay is a universal quality, like cooking, like decorating the body, like singing, like predicting the weather. Moreover, after learning about the social positions and special offices fulfilled by Indians whose tribes once picked them for the tasks of naming, healing, prediction, leadership, and teaching precisely because they displayed characteristics we call gay, I knew that Gayness goes far beyond simple sexual/emotional activity. What Americans call Gayness not only has distinct cultural characteristics, its participants have long held positions of social power in history and ritual among people all over the globe.

—Judy Grahn, *Another Mother Tongue*

CONTENTS

LIST OF ILLUSTRATIONS

ACKNOWLEDGMENTS

The Board of Directors of Gay American Indians would like to honor the contributions of many individuals who made this project possible.

Will Roscoe has volunteered his services to the History Project since its inception in 1984 and has been the coordinating editor for *Living the Spirit.*

Paula Gunn Allen, Evie Blackwood, Maya Chuma, Tevia Clark, Harry Hay, Howard Junker, Maurice Kenny, Owlfeather, and Mark Thompson provided invaluable advice and encouragement. Beth Brant and Anne Waters helped review submissions.

Joaquin Arriaga and Tom Lippert located source materials, and Joseph Agonito shared historical photographs.

Gerald Stilwell made a timely financial donation. The Bay Area Center for Art and Technology served as our fiscal sponsor. The Chicago Resource Center and the Golden Gate Business Association provided grants.

We also recognize the contributions of Board members and volunteers, past and present, who have kept the GAI spirit alive all these years.

And, of course, we acknowledge all the brothers and sisters who have chosen to stand with us—our contributors. Thanks to their generosity, all proceeds from *Living the Spirit: A Gay American Indian Anthology* will benefit GAI's programs and services.

PREFACE

RANDY BURNS
NORTHERN PAIUTE

When the U.S. Supreme Court cited "millennia of moral teaching" in support of Georgia's sodomy law and when the Vatican declared homosexuality "intrinsically evil," they must not have been thinking of American history and American morals. Because, throughout America, for centuries before and after the arrival of Europeans, gay and lesbian American Indians were recognized and valued members of tribal communities. As Maurice Kenny declares, "We were special!"

Our tribes occupied every region of this continent, and our cultures were diverse and rich—from the hunters of the far North, to the trading people of the Northwest Coast, the farmers and city-builders of the Southwest, the hunters of the plains, and the great confederations of the Northeast.

Gay American Indians were a part of all these communities. We lived openly in our tribes. Our families and communities recognized us and encouraged us to develop our skills. In turn, we made special contributions to our communities.

French explorers used the word *berdache* to describe male Indians who specialized in the work of women and formed emotional and sexual relationships with other men. Many tribes had female berdaches, too—women who took on men's work and married other women. The History Project of Gay American Indians (GAI) has documented these alternative roles in over 135 North American tribes (see the list of tribes in part 3).

As artists, providers, and healers, our traditional gay ancestors had important responsibilities.

Women hunters and warriors brought food for their families and defended their communities, like the famous Kutenai woman warrior who became an intertribal courier and a prophet in the early 1800s, or Woman Chief of the Crow Indians, who achieved the third highest rank in her tribe. Among the Mohave, lesbian women became powerful shamans and medicine people.

Male berdaches specialized in the arts and crafts of their tribes and performed important social and religious roles. In California, we were often called upon to bury and mourn the dead, because such close contact with the spirit world was considered too dangerous for others. Among the Navajo, berdaches were healers and artists, while among the Plains Indians, we were famous for the valuable crafts we made.

Gay and lesbian American Indians today represent the continuity of this tradition. We are living in the spirit of our gay Indian ancestors. Much has changed in American Indian life, but we are still here, a part of our communities, struggling to face the realities of contemporary life.

Some of us continue to fill traditional roles in our tribal communities; others are artists, healers, mediators, and community organizers in urban areas; many of us are active in efforts to restore and preserve our cultural traditions.

Gay and lesbian Indians were special to a lot of tribes. We have roots here in North America.

At the same time, gay American Indians face *double oppression*—both racism and homophobia.

As Indians, our cultural and economic survival is threatened by poverty, poor education, and unemployment. Many American Indians have left reservations for urban areas (where nearly 50 percent of Indians live today). But in the cities, we find racial prejudice, discrimination, and denial of education, job training, employment, and housing.

In fact, racial discrimination is not limited to the nongay community. In 1983 GAI participated in hearings sponsored by the San Francisco Human Rights Commission that documented discrimination against nonwhite people within the lesbian/gay community itself. Even now, leadership roles in the gay community continue to be filled by white males, and minority tokenism is the rule. Organizations are always coming to GAI, eager for Indian representation—but they fail to address the economic and social obstacles to equal and full participation, and they ignore our input when we do participate.

At the same time, we face oppression as gay people, too, sometimes within our own Indian communities. In 1975, when we were organizing GAI, the local American Indian center refused to post our flyers because they might "offend" people. When we participated in an American Indian Day held at a local university, we were told to take down our booth: "We don't want any trouble," they said.

Back then, we expected to receive negative remarks, from not only the non-Indian community but from our Indian counterparts, as well. Unfortunately, Indian homophobia is still a problem today.

Many Indian agencies now eager to receive AIDS funding have been antigay for years. Gay Indian parents must fight long court battles for the custody of their children. Members of our community, some who are pipe-bearers themselves, have been excluded from Sun Dances—even though, among some tribes, finding and cutting the center pole for the ceremony was a traditional gay role! On reservations, gay and lesbian Indians face rejection and harassment.

This is not surprising, however, considering the efforts of Indian agents, missionaries, and boarding schools to suppress all forms of traditional Indian culture. Many Indian people have been taught to be ashamed of such roles as the berdache. Indian leaders, even traditionalists, have adopted the attitudes of white society toward gay people. Only the elders remember, but in the face of violent homophobia they have been reluctant to speak up.

Gay American Indians was founded in 1975 by Randy Burns (Northern Paiute) and Barbara Cameron (Lakota Sioux) to serve the needs and interests of the gay American Indian community. We came together then to share a common identity, to give and receive emotional support, and to share our rich heritage as American Indians. We were the first gay Indian organization in the United States.

Many of us had never lived in cities. We came from reservations across the country. Our older gay brothers and sisters had come to places like San Francisco in the 1950s as part of the Bureau of Indian Affairs' relocation program. In the 1970s many of us moved to cities to receive higher education and training. We were young, and our dream was to return someday to our reservations and help our people—and many of us have returned.

GAI grew beyond our wildest dreams. We've gone a long way in challenging double oppression and ending the isolation of gay Indians. GAI's programs include referral services, cultural and educational projects, and active involvement within local networks of Indian organizations and agencies. Today we have one thousand Indian and non-Indian members. The unity of men and women from many different tribes within GAI is based on our unique heritage as American Indians and our mutual respect for individual tribal customs and traditions.

In 1984 we formed the Gay American Indian History Project, to collect information on our history and to make it available to the larger community. The History Project has compiled an extensive bibliography of sources on berdache and alternative gender roles, edited by Will Roscoe and published by the *Journal of Homosexuality* (see sources), and it has coordinated the development of this anthology.

Today GAI is active in education and training programs related to the AIDS crisis (the Acquired Immune Deficiency Syndrome). Here, again, we face the challenge of double oppression. As gay people, our health needs are not taken seriously by the government. As Indians, we often find that AIDS programs overlook important cultural differences and fail to reach many Indian people. Many agencies do not even have statistics on the Indians they serve, or they count us in the "other/unknown" category. We are working to change this situation by educating and training our own community about AIDS, and educating AIDS funding sources and service providers about the needs of Indian people.

Above all, GAI has become an extended family for gay Indians—not only those of us who live in the San Francisco Bay area, but for our many family and friends who regularly visit from other areas, as well. GAI has re-created the kinship ties of the traditional Indian family in an urban setting, and this has made all of us stronger.

Gay American Indians are active members of both the American Indian and gay communities. But our voices have not been heard. To end this silence, GAI is publishing *Living the Spirit: A Gay American Indian Anthology.*

Living the Spirit honors the past and present life of gay American Indians. This book is not just *about* gay American Indians, it is *by* gay Indians. Over twenty different American Indian writers, men and women, represent tribes from every part of North America.

Living the Spirit tells our story—the story of our history and traditions, as well as the realities and challenges of the present.

As Paula Gunn Allen writes, "Some like Indians endure." The themes of change and continuity are a part of every contribution in this book—in the contemporary coyote tales by Daniel-Harry Steward and Beth Brant—in the reservation experiences of Owlfeather and Erna Pahe—in the gay urban experiences of Jerry, a Hupa Indian—in the painful memories of cruelty and injustice that Beth Brant, Chrystos, and others evoke. Our pain, but also our joy, our love, and our sexuality, are all here, in these pages.

Owlfeather writes, "If traditions have been lost, then new ones should be borrowed from other tribes," and he uses the example of the Indian pow-wow—Indian, yet contemporary and pantribal.

One of our traditional roles was that of "go-between"—individuals who could help different groups communicate with each other. This is the role GAI hopes to play today. We are advocates for not only gay but American Indian concerns, as well. We are turning double oppression into a double opportunity—the chance to build bridges between communities, to create a place for gay Indians in both of the worlds we live in, to honor our past and secure our future.

PART ONE

ARTISTS, HEALERS, AND PROVIDERS

THE BERDACHE HERITAGE

Metropolitan Indian Series, 1982.
Hulleah Tsinhnahjinnie.

PAULA GUNN ALLEN
LAGUNA PUEBLO/SIOUX

SOME LIKE INDIANS ENDURE

i have it in my mind that
dykes are indians

they're a lot like indians
they used to live as tribes
they owned tribal land
it was called the earth

they were massacred
lots of times
they always came back
like the grass
like the clouds
they got massacred again

they thought caringsharing
about the earth and each other
was a good thing
they rode horses
and sang to the moon

but i don't know
about what was so longago
and it's now that dykes
make me think i'm with indians
when i'm with dykes

because they bear
witness bitterly
because they reach
and hold
because they live every day
with despair laughing
in cities and country places
because earth hides them
because they know
the moon

because they gather together
enclosing
and spit in the eye of death

indian is an idea
some people have
of themselves
dyke is an idea some women
have of themselves
the place where we live now
is idea
because whiteman took
all the rest
because father
took all the rest
but the idea which
once you have it
you can't be taken
for somebody else
and have nowhere to go
like indians you can be
stubborn

the idea might move you on,
ponydrag behind
taking all your loves and
children maybe downstream

maybe beyond the cliffs
but it hangs in there
an idea
like indians
endures

it might even take your
whole village with it
stone by stone
or leave the stones
and find more
to build another village
someplace else

like indians
dykes have fewer and fewer
someplace elses to go
so it gets important
to know
about ideas and
to remember or uncover
the past
and how the people
traveled
all the while remembering
the idea they had
about who they were
indians, like dykes
do it all the time

dykes know all about dying
and that everything belongs
to the wind
like indians
they do terrible things
to each other
out of sheer cussedness
out of forgetting
out of despair

so dykes
are like indians
because everybody is related
to everybody
in pain
in terror
in guilt
in blood
in shame
in disappearance
that never quite manages
to be disappeared
we never go away
even if we're always
leaving

because the only home
is each other
they've occupied all
the rest
colonized it; an
idea about ourselves is all
we own

and dykes remind me of indians
like indians   dykes
are supposed to die out
or forget
or drink all the time
or shatter
go away
to nowhere
to remember what will happen
if they don't

they don't anyway—even
though the worst happens

they remember and they
stay
because the moon remembers
because so does the sun
because the stars
remember
and the persistent stubborn grass
of the earth

Berdache, 18x24, tempera on bristol, 1987.
Joe Lawrence Lembo.

MAURICE KENNY
MOHAWK

TINSELLED BUCKS: A HISTORICAL STUDY IN INDIAN HOMOSEXUALITY

Upon coming to the New World, Spain loosed an army of priests upon the Indians to take souls for God and gold for King. The sexual practices of the natives have not been recorded by anthropology. Anything that smacked of heathenism, religion, art, or sex was thoroughly destroyed. It must be recalled that pleasure-sex was branded "wrong" by civilized Europeans. Male love was destroyed more than ignored in the macho Spanish New World.

The French Jesuits, who first explored northeastern America, did not chronicle overt manifestations of homosexuality within the tribes they met. Nor did the Dutch, English, or Puritans. Homosexuality, being against God, king, and nature, would be a vile, repulsive subject for official record. Consequently New World writings mostly ignore any manifestation of male love in the natives of the new land. Distortion and outright lies were used early in American history. Where can the data be found, in what record can it be discovered that the lonesome cowboy or the restricted soldier of the U.S. cavalry ever indulged in male love? Yet it may be easily assumed that cowboys and soldiers practiced homosexuality. Even America's legendary heroes fall under suspicion. Mike Fink, the famous riverman, is said to have killed his young friend, Carpenter, out of a consuming fit of jealousy.

Though there are rare suggestions in the old chronicles or journals that the early mountainmen habitually cohabited with each other, or Indian males, probably the human shredding machine was early put to work. It is easy to propose that there existed a sexual fraternity at certain times. For the hardy mountaineer

Reprinted, with changes, from Gay Sunshine *26/27 (Winter 1975–1976, pp. 15–17).*

masturbation would not have been sufficiently gratifying. Sex with a female was completely accepted, but there might have been some sticky embarrassment were it known the mountaineer seduced the band's young males, as well. This would suggest effeminacy to the Indian, and as Paul Radin suggested, "It is not the charge of effeminacy he fears but the possibility of being ridiculed" (Radin 1963:45). This quote, however, does not prove there was no sexual activity between whites and Indian males.

In some tribes, it has been said that Indian women lived miserable lives and were sometimes known to commit suicide to rid themselves of their abject bondage to a merciless husband. A young man might also commit suicide on discovering he had no incentive to the warpath but did have tendencies toward homosexuality, or had a physical handicap that would negate the possibility of attaining honor as a warrior. The threat of donning the garb ("one who wears skirts") and duty of females could definitely throw him into depression, making him fear rejection and ridicule.

In general, however, the Indian attitude toward sex was not constricting:

> Compared to white attitudes toward sex, Indians were utterly uninhibited. They suffered no embarrassment.... Adults coupled freely in front of their children or anyone else. One prominent chief was often seen walking about his village naked, displaying an erection. ... And the American Indian was completely innocent of the notion that something he enjoyed might be "wrong." "Wrong" would have been an incomprehensible concept to them in that context. (Blevins 1973:215–16)

Homosexuality is accepted if not condoned within most primal societies. In certain societies the homosexual was made a fetish or became an integral part of ceremony. The American Indian was no exception to the rule. He used the role as an advantage to obtain lovers. Ruth Benedict, in reference to the Zuni Indians of New Mexico, wrote in her book *Patterns of Culture:*

> Social scorn, however, was not visited upon the berdache but upon the man he chose to live with him. The latter was regarded as a weak

> man who had chosen an easy berth instead of the recognized goals of their culture; he did not contribute to the household, which was already a model for all households through the sole efforts of the berdache. His sexual adjustment was not singled out in the judgment that was passed upon him, but in terms of his economic adjustment he was an outcast. (1959: 264–65)

The cult of the berdache was more known on the western plains within the Sioux (Lakota) and Cheyenne tribes west of the Mississippi than in other areas of America. There is no particularly good reason why this should be true other than the possibility that these were large and powerful tribes before the white man decimated their numbers. Within such large groups a social-religious use could be found for the berdache. As there were sufficient warriors and hunters to both protect and feed the community, some males were allowed to pursue more gentle endeavors. A more leisurely society could afford such deviations from the straight path of war and the hunt, as medicine men to provide the stimulus of religion, and as artisans. A youth not inclined to the warpath or game hunting might spend his life in pursuit of other careers and was not necessarily required to propagate the race. The tribe could afford to allow a youth the lifestyle of a berdache. In the Southwest, along with slavery, homosexuality was also known and condoned in such tribes as the Navajo and Mojave. "The conspicuous transvestism of the Mojave—where the transvestite men mimic pregnancy and childbirth, going aside from the camp to be ceremonially delivered of stones" attests to its presence in the desert lands (Mead 1949:129). The Far West, the South, and the Northeast certainly were not without such personages.

It is known that the Indian berdache sometimes married their own sex and lived together, and the "husband" was not always a fellow invert. Throughout any discussion of Indian homosexuality it must be remembered that the cardinal aim and fulfillment of Indian males was the attainment of honor and glory on the warpath. From birth this was instilled and impressed daily upon his mind. Masculine strength was the protector of life and liberty; the provider-hunter sustained the people, and procreation was the basic sexual drive. If too many "faint hearts" were allowed to survive, the tribe and culture were doomed. For this reason small boys were sometimes taken from the mother, who might shed too much love and attention and sway the teetering balance of a boy's potential inversion, at a very early age, usually before they attained five years. In some Indian nations, the male child was given to an uncle to rear in the respected masculine custom and Indian way. This was a safeguard to eliminate the possibility that a boy would turn from the warrior and hunter's gun. Needless to say, occasionally a male slipped through this protective measure and matured a berdache to denounce the warpath and accept female clothes and drudgery. Not all males could meet the high Indian standards. Along with the invert, physically malformed men were often obliged to assume maiden ways.

Homosexuality was found in all American Indian tribes, though perhaps it was kept to a small number in particular tribes. A childhood "puberty vision" may well have placed this onus upon a young man's head or predilection in his nature. A number of males who practiced homosexuality were fierce warriors and were not effeminate, transvestite homoerotics. Bestiality was sometimes practiced, and sex with a recently killed enemy was not frowned upon in certain tribes. What greater ridicule or humiliation in defeat could be put upon a foe! His macho powers would be weakened in the Spirit World. The berdache, unlike captives and especially women, rarely suffered the experience of rape and the act of being "passed on the plains"—that is, attacked *en masse*—as a consequence of being an invert.

Alexander Henry the Younger, a trapper-trader, was an early chronicler of the Indian lifestyle, despite his aversion to the red man. In 1801 Henry wrote of "La Berdash" and left a description: "This person is a curious compound between a man and a woman. He is a man both to members and courage, but pretends to be womanish, and dresses as such. His walk and mode of sitting, his manners, occupations, and language are those of a woman. His father, who is a great chief amongst the Saulteurs, cannot persuade him to act like a man" (1897:163).

In 1864 a young cavalry officer, Lt. Eugene F. Ware, wrote that the entire population of the male Poncas was effeminate, and their females masculine, mainly because the males seemed to be

> kindly, lazy, inefficient.... They seemed to have small feet and to be more feminine than the women.... The squaws all appeared to be of such fiber that they could trounce their husbands easily, and throw them out of the tent when they wanted to.... I think that some of the contempt which the early settlers had for the Indian was due to his effeminate actions and appearance. In addition to this, the Indian grew no whiskers, and had a general inefficient manner, and was not in stature and build the equal of the white boys that were in our company. (1960:28)

This nonsense was written by a man who could also write that the white man was not only smarter than the Indian in civilization but also in the wilderness while competing with the Indian, and "The Indians were a wild, bloodthirsty set of barbarians, and one half, at least, of them deserved killing as much as the wolves which barked around their tepees" (147). This was commonly thought on the plains during the days of the great western migrations. Can a man who reflects this sheer insanity be trusted for accuracy? His bias is no more sound than contemporary invectives leveled against homosexuals or any socially acknowledged minority.

In her book *Male and Female,* Margaret Mead writes of the berdache: "Among many American Indian tribes the berdache, the man who dressed and lived as a woman, was a recognized social institution, counterpointed to the excessive emphasis upon bravery and hardiness for men" (1949:129).

The berdache was known by different names to different tribes. Catlin, the painter, recorded that the Sauk and Fox tribes called the berdache *i-coo-coo-a;* the Ojibwa (Chippewa) named him *agokwa;* the Cheyenne, according to George Bird Grinnell, called him *hee-man-eh;* and the Sioux, *winkte.*

Certain berdaches were celebrated, and their names and exploits have come down to us. Henry the Younger and Walter O'Meara mention Yellow Head of the Ojibway; George Bent informed anthropologist George B. Grinnell of several old Cheyenne: Pipe, Bridge (also mentioned by Mari Sandoz in *Cheyenne Autumn),* Hiding Shield Under His Robe, and Good Road Woman—names somewhat indicative of their proclivities. Stanley Vestal, the noted historian, wrote favorably, though amusingly, of a famed Arapaho medicine man, Waksenna, and how he saved his band from Asiatic cholera. Ruth Benedict refers to Matilda Coxe Stevenson's Zuni friend, We'wha.

The berdache was often the tribe or band's medicine man, doctor, story teller, matchmaker, or leading scalp dancer. He functioned within the tribe. He was *sometimes* educated as a medicine man (holy man), as certain taboos in particular tribes forbade their high priest to marry women and father children. Within the Cheyenne tribe the Contrary, or Bow String, Society, a warrior group that did everything backward, had to abstain from marriage with a female. This could only lead to male love. Roman Nose, the famous Cheyenne Dog Soldier warrior, was thought to have been unmarried because a medicine man forbade it. The taboo required that Roman Nose not copulate with a female as it would not only anger the water spirits who were very close to Roman Nose's "medicine bundle"—it would weaken if not totally destroy his warrior prowess. Later, however, Cheyenne half-breed George Bent attested that Roman Nose had at least one wife and child.

Every American Indian tribe had its fetishes and taboos, but no tribe had ironclad laws that said a young man need take this or that path; he made up his own mind and followed the direction of his "puberty vision," his inclination, though the tribal mores prodded him toward the warrior-hunter career. If a youth chose not to go on the hunt or join a warrior society then he need not comply with the general pattern and war or hunt. But in his choice of not warring, he was usually compelled to forfeit his right to masculine privilege. He also possibly exposed himself to insulting ridicule and abuse though rarely would he have been castigated, ostracized, or expelled from the encampment. Should he decide war paint was against his basic nature, he could dress as a female and take her occupations. He might even become the second or third wife to a warrior or chief, should the benefactor possess sufficient wealth to support an addition to his lodge.

According to George Catlin, the Mandan berdache easily found such a person who killed his meat and hunted hides for his clothing. Catlin, who apparently was not deeply disturbed by the presence of berdaches in the Mandan villages, has left a long description of these young dandies. Once, excited by a young man's attire and countenance, Catlin painted a Mandan dandy. He destroyed the portrait before completion at the insistence of an indignant chief who had had his portrait done earlier. In his *Letters and Notes* Catlin wrote:

> So highly do Mandan braves and worthies value the honour of being painted; and so little do they value a man, however lavishly Nature may have bestowed her master touch upon him, who has not the pride and noble bearing of a warrior . . .
>
> . . . These clean and elegant gentlemen, who are few in each tribe, are held in very little estimation by the chiefs and braves; inasmuch as it is known by all, that they have a most horrible aversion to arms, and are denominated "faint hearts" and "old women" by the whole tribe, and are therefore but little respected. They seem, however, to be tolerably well contented with the appellation, together with the celebrity they have acquired amongst the women and children for the beauty and elegance of their personal appearance. . . .
>
> *These gay and tinselled bucks* [my italics] may be seen in a pleasant day in all their plumes, astride of their pied or dappled ponies, with a fan in the right hand, made of a turkey's tail—with a whip and fly-brush attached to the wrist of the same hand, and underneath them a white and beautiful and soft pleasure-saddle, ornamented with porcupine quills and ermine, parading through or lounging about the village. . . .
>
> There was nought about him of the terrible, and nought to shock the finest, chastest intellect. (1973a:112–13)

Perhaps Catlin appreciated the berdache more than the Mandan Indians did. Although the Mandan may not have valued the berdache highly, they did respect the homosexual sufficiently that he was neither tortured by confinement nor driven to suicide, though surely humorous pranks must have been played upon him and epithets or ridicule applied.

Not all tribes held an aversion to the berdache. In the Navajo myths a male hermaphrodite, Turquoise Boy, played a significant role in the Creation. He became masculine and was known as the Bearer of the Sun. The Bearer of the Moon, White Shell Girl, was also a hermaphrodite. While still a hermaphrodite, Turquoise Boy saved the ancient Navajos from the angry Water Buffalo who stood in their way between evolving from the Fourth to the Fifth and final world. "The Turquoise Hermaphrodite was the first man to change, or become, as a woman. . . . First Woman and the Turquoise Hermaphrodite represented the female principle" (O'Bryan 1956:6–7).

In the Winnebago tales of the prankish Trickster (often described as a coyote) there are references to transvestism. In one tale the male Trickster changes into a woman and marries a chief's son and bears children, having had intercourse first with "the fox, the jaybird, and the nit," as well as with the young human brave:

> Immediately they prepared dried corn for her and they boiled slit bear-ribs. That was why the Trickster was getting married, of course. . . . One day later, as they were steaming corn, the chief's wife teased her sister-in-law. She chased her around the pit where they were steaming corn. Finally, the chief's son's wife (Trickster) jumped over the pit and she dropped something very rotten. The people shouted at her, "It is Trickster!" The men were all ashamed, especially the chief's son. The animals who had been with Trickster, the fox, the jaybird, and the nit, all of them now ran away. (Radin 1972:23–24)

Trickster was often a very naughty, saucy fellow who carried his penis in a large box on his back, and many of his picaresque adventures dealt in scatological farce—naturally, with a moral tied to the fable. Trickster often overprotected his penis, anus, and feces, and though they sometimes afforded him much pleasure and gratification, his penis and anus brought about humorous disaster.

Even Lewis and Clark on their westerly exploration of Jefferson's Louisiana Purchase were confronted, but undisturbed, by berdaches. During the ferocious winter of 1804 they were encamped between the Mississippi and the Missouri rivers near a Mandan village. They were approached by "a number of Squars and men Dressed in Squars Clothes [who] Came with Corn to sell to the men for little things" (DeVoto 1953:74).

Only a handful of years later, Catlin admiringly wrote of the "Dance to the *Berdashe*," as celebrated by the Sioux and the Sauk and Fox Indians:

> Dance to the *Berdashe* is a very funny and amusing scene, which happens once a year or oftener, as they choose, when a feast is given to the *"Berdashe,"* as he is called in French (or *I-coo-coo-a,* in their own language), who is a man dressed in woman's clothes, as he is known to be all his life, and for extraordinary privileges which he is known to possess, he is driven to the most servile and degrading duties, which he is not allowed to escape; and he being the only one of the tribe submitting to this disgraceful degradation, is looked upon as medicine and sacred, and a feast is given him annually; and initiatory to it, a dance by those few young men of the tribe who can, as in the sketch, dance forward and publicly make their boast (without the denial of the Berdashe), that. . . . (1973b:214–5)

Here follow three untranslatable lines in the Indian language.

George Grinnell also describes at great length the ceremony of the Cheyenne scalp dance, for which he pays tribute to George Bent as informant:

> These old time scalp dances were directed by a little group of men called *Hee man eh',* "halfmen-halfwomen," who usually dressed as old men. . . . They were very popular and especial favorites of the young people, whether married or not, for they were noted matchmakers. They were fine love talkers. If a man wanted to get a girl to run away with him and could get one of these people to help him, he seldom failed. When a young man wanted to send gifts for a young woman, one of these halfmen-halfwomen was sent to the girl's relative to do the talking in making the marriage. . . .
>
> When a war party was preparing to start out, one of these persons was often asked to accompany it, and, in fact, in old times large war parties rarely started without one or two of them. They were good company and fine talkers. When they went with the war parties they were well treated. They watched all that was being done, and in the fighting cared for the wounded, in which they were skillful, for they were doctors or medicine men. (1923:39–40)

They were probably also assigned the task of disemboweling the enemy dead and emasculating the prone corpses.

It is easily understood why a *hee-man-eh,* or halfman-halfwoman, would be chosen as leader of the scalp dance and to officiate as bearer of the scalps to the village. He had special powers, or privileged medicine, and for all intents and purposes he had if not the outer apparel then the inner spirit of both male and female. He was also clean of the menstrual taboo. Mountain Wolf Woman, a Winnebago, related in her autobiography that while in her period a woman "should not look at anyone, not even a glance. If you look at a man you will contaminate his blood. Even a glance will cause you to be an evil person" (Lurie 1973:22).

In his book *The Cheyennes,* E. Adamson Hoebel suggests that the fact that enemy scalps were given to the *hee-man-eh* "indicates that warriors feel their success is due to the presence of these personages" in victorious battle. "War parties like to have Halfmen-halfwomen along, not only for their medical skill, but because they are socially graceful and entertaining" (1960:77).

A note might be added here that women were rarely taken on war parties. They were left in the village because, mainly, should a menstrual flow come upon a woman, her blood might very well bring defeat upon the party due to her impurity. A series of long purification rites would result, causing delay that could end in dishonorable defeat. Males lived in great fear of the female process. As females did not accompany the war party, a *hee-man-eh* would easily serve for sexual entertainments, as it was well known to the elders that young hot-headed braves' frustration might result in either a disorderly attack or a sophomoric group raiding an enemy for first honors before the war chief could assemble the more mature and total war party. Young men, especially those courting maidens, were constantly running off from the main party to count first coup and take honors to lay at their lovers' feet for her respect and eventually her hand in marriage. No young girl wished to marry a brave who came to her without war honors, a first feather, or a proud wound. Hence the potential need of a *hee-man-eh* to cool youthful foolishness.

Colonel Richard Irving Dodge, in the 1880s, wrote also of a special social dance during which a pretty girl of the Cheyenne village had captivated the eyes and hearts of most attending males. Dodge subtitles the episode "A Delicious Bit of Masquerading": "Finally, a young buck with whom she was dancing discovered that 'she' was a boy dressed in his sister's clothing. The little rascal had played his part so well as to mystify the whole party for half the night, and with so pretty, sprightly, and natural an action, that half the bucks in the dance had made love to him. It was considered a wonderful feat, and made great sport" (1883:377). Dodge wrote, as did Paul Radin, that the male Indian considered affection effeminate.

Other than in contemporary novels, there is little in the old journals, chronicles, histories, or anthropological studies relating to lovemaking between two Indian males. But the many references to the berdache would certainly indicate that copulation was practiced.

Walter O'Meara cites an example of unrequited love between a young Ojibwa *agokwa* (berdache) and the mountaineer John Tanner. He was Yellow Head, the same *agokwa* who had so greatly perturbed Alexander Henry the Younger.

One winter while Tanner was encamped at a post on Red River in the central north, a son of a celebrated Ojibwa (Chippewa) chief visited the post. Tanner termed him a "creature." He claimed that most, if not all, Indian tribes had *agokwas.* The Ojibwa accepted the berdache. Yellow Head took a fancy to the white man and set his stars upon capturing Tanner as his lover. To Tanner, who had sometime before married an Indian maid and sired children by her, the "creature" was a loathsome object. The *agokwa* offered himself to Tanner, and he was not discouraged by the mountaineer's rejection. The females of the post took great amusement in this odd affair and, most likely, prodded the *agokwa* to further and more intimate advances, which Tanner spurned and nipped in the bud. Yellow Head disappeared for a few days. Tanner felt tremendous relief and decided he had finally chased the "creature" off. But the berdache returned to the post later with a pack horse loaded with fresh meat. At that time the post was low on supplies, especially fresh meat, and the people were hungry. Normally under those circumstances meat would have gained a hunter access to a maid's lodge and bed. But neither fresh meat nor the hunter's prowess won Yellow Head Tanner's love or male body. Yellow Head, the *agokwa,* received instead total rejection for his generous and strenuous efforts. A solution was discovered at last. The chief, Wagetote, already served by two wives, married the *agokwa.* Tanner was saved from his embarrassment and the trauma of either ridding himself of the determined berdache or accepting Yellow Head into his lodge as concubine or wife. But love between two males, of either race, was not always unrequited. It can be assumed that there were exceptions that led to romance and marriage. All males did not have Tanner's aversion to *agokwas* and the comforts they might bring to a tired warrior-hunter (O'Meara 1962:165–67).

According to Alexander Henry, Yellow Head, when drunk, was not merely a nuisance but a bothersome man (1897:164). Yet Henry Rowe Schoolcraft, who had personally known the *agokwa,* reported that Yellow Head was very courageous in battle (1834), and Henry himself told of Yellow Head's exploits and daring on the warpath. According to O'Meara, "He was famous for having once stood off a whole band of Sioux with nothing but a bow and arrows, while he covered his companions' retreat to safety" (1962:167–68).

Even when he sometimes wore female garb, the berdache was not always a fluttering "sissy." John Major Hurdy wrote in his book *American Indian Religion:*

> However, the desire to copulate with one's sex is by no means connected, as army men in every culture have witnessed, with timidity in battle. . . . Society worked effectively to prevent individual guilt, so also its structure mitigated against the development of machoism. . . . Lakota males have been known to commit suicide rather than accept the fate their vision and inner reactions told them was theirs. . . . The degree of physical courage, superb skill, and keen competitive spirit demanded by the masculine ideal was so high that not all males were capable of conforming to it. Those who were clumsy or weak, or were cursed with sluggish reflexes, rarely survived to become problems as adults. And for those who cringed at violence, Sioux society provided an escape route. (1970:48–49)

Toleration of the berdache varied from tribe to tribe. Some tribes, such as the Illinois, actually trained young men to become homosexuals and concubines of men. The Cheyenne and Sioux of the plains may not have purposely trained young men to become berdaches but certainly accepted homosexuals more readily than perhaps other tribes.

A number of contemporary novels, such as Thomas Berger's excellent *Little Big Man,* a satire of the West, treat romance between Indian males. Berger's satire fails only because he himself became entangled with his characters and took *too serious* an interest in their lives and conflicts, even probably those of the young *hee-man-eh,* Little Horse, who Berger stripped of masculine attire and lifestyle and costumed in a female's deerskin tunic. Berger gave Little Horse a husband and a certain amount of joy in the union. Even though placed in the novel for comic relief, Little Horse fared better than most of the other, principal characters, including the hero, Jack Crabb. *Little Big Man,* an important major novel of the twentieth century, is a highly researched account of Cheyenne life and death during the mid-1800s. Though Berger's satire is not completely satisfactory, his power of vision is ovewhelming, his humor delightfully entertaining, and his characters' conflicts humanly moving:

> If a Cheyenne don't believe he can stand a man's life, he ain't forced to. He can become a *heemaneh,* which is to say half-man, half-woman. There are uses for these fellows and everybody likes them. They are sometimes chemists, specializing in making of the love-potions, and generally good entertainers. They wear women's clothes and can get married to another man, if such be his taste. . . . (1964:76–77)

> My other foster-brother, Little Horse, dressed like a Cheyenne woman, came in and entertained us with very graceful singing and dancing. It did my heart good to see he made such a success of being a *heemaneh.* (169)

Little Horse chose to marry Younger Bear of the Contraries, or the Bowstring Warrior Society. The Contrary warriors were a very special society. If in the "puberty vision" a youth is visited by the Thunderbirds (Hawks)—and it is the intercession of this sign that designates a boy's future occupation within the tribal arts of war, hunt, medicine, and so on—he becomes a suicidal warrior. He may not marry a female. If he does marry he must forfeit his lance, inherent with sexual symbolism that suggests the male sex organ tied and restrained. Every thought, word, and action he commits must be accomplished backward. If in reality he is hungry he must feel contented. He bathes in sand and dries off with water. He cries when he is happy and laughs when sorrowful. He rejects heterosexuality. He is obliged, by taboo and his society, to do everything in opposites. In this rejection of heterosexuality, "the Contrary rejects normal social relations. He must live alone, apart from all the camp. . . . Even in battle, he cannot charge with the other warriors at his side or in front or behind him. He must be off on the flanks, alone. When he holds his Thunder Bow (lance) in his right hand, he may not retreat" (Hoebel 1960:97). There were usually only two or three Contraries to a band, deviates in their own right, often accompanied by *hee-man-ehs*.

In his book *The Cheyennes,* Hoebel writes: "We put these two facts together and suggest the following: the Contraries, like the Halfmen-halfwomen, are neurotically anxious about sex relations and their own virility. Whereas, the Halfmen-halfwomen find refuge in total rejection of male sexuality, the Contraries seek validation in an exaggerated male rejection of heterosexuality" (1960:97).

Berger's *hee-man-eh,* Little Horse, married such a young Contrary. Younger Bear sold his Thunder-Bow, which allowed marriage between them. Berger cannot resist a play for humor, a stab at jest: "So when the Bear was all dressed and looking at me, I couldn't forbear from needling him a little, for though *nobody among the Cheyenne ever condemns a* hee-man-eh [my italics], it is O.K. to rib the fellow he lives with" (1964:227).

In one stroke Berger sums up the Cheyenne traditional attitude toward homosexuality and transvestism. His conclusion may very well speak for other Indian tribes, as well. The contemporary Cheyenne, especially a reservation-oriented Cheyenne, might not accept Berger's statement. The modern Indian has been programmed by white society so that his former mores and measurements have been changed to fit his ever-assimilating environment. With the loss of his religious rites and culture, there is probably no place for the contemporary *hee-man-eh* within that social structure. There are no warriors to entertain on the warpath; no scalps to dance over; no mountaineers to court, subdue, and copulate with; and certainly no ceremonial dances exclusively devoted to the berdache. Many traditionalists have become racist and sexist, and are generally disquieted when among homosexuals. Hollywood, TV, and the church have had a heavy influence on the changing attitude of Indian thought. Berger was writing fictionally of a "romantic" past, and, though accurately researched, *Little Big Man* may represent one man's point of view. Perhaps even today, the reservation Indian still fears the possibility of ridicule, as Paul Radin suggested in reference to his Winnebago at the turn of the century. Though a homosexual may not be a Trickster, he is in certain quarters regarded as a buffoon to be laughed at, mimicked, jeered, and even possibly scorned.

Frederick Manfred, in his western novels, has various references to homosexuality, again in a humorous, jesting vein, or as a curse or epithet spat by a female upon her lazy husband. In *Lord Grizzly,* Manfred refers to a berdache as he who "Can't Father" (1954:30).

Non-Indians, or Anglos, were not the only writers on male love in Indian societies. The Indian himself wrote, though often with the help, aid, and tape recorders of such white men as John G. Neihardt, who was responsible for the important story of the holy man, Black Elk, and Thomas B. Marquis, who helped direct the Cheyenne warrior Wooden Leg to express his life story. Richard Erdoes taped and edited the life of the Lakota medicine man John Fire, or Lame Deer, an old man still living in 1972 when his book, *Lame Deer Seeker of Visions,* was first published.

John Lame Deer, with Erdoes, stopped for a drink in a country bar. Near them on a stool sat a man, obviously "gay." Lame Deer opened a conversation with the man, a *winkte,* as the Sioux call male homosexuals.

> He told me that a *winkte* has a gift of prophecy and that he himself could predict the weather. . . . In our tribe we go to a *winkte* to give a newborn child a secret name. . . . A name given by a *winkte* is supposed to bring its bearer luck and long life. In the old days it was worth a fine horse—at the least. . . .
>
> We think if a woman has two little ones growing inside of her, if she is going to have twins, sometimes instead of giving birth to two babies they have formed up in her womb into just one, into a half

> man-half woman kind of being. We call such a person a *winkte*. He could be a hermaphrodite with male and female parts. . . . To us a man is what nature, or his dreams, makes him. We accept him for what he wants to be. That's up to him. Still, fathers did not like to see their boys hanging around a *winkte's* place and told them to stay away. (1972:149–50)

The Sioux *winkte* still exists. As the half man–half woman that Lame Deer spoke with said, "If nature puts a burden on a man by making him different, it also gives him a power" (1972:149).

The Sioux had an old custom of giving themselves secret names divulged to no one. Only the donor and the recipient knew the name. The name given by the *winkte* is sort of a good-luck talisman, and apparently the names received are "very sexy, even funny, very outspoken" (1972:150). Were they to be known they would cause embarrassment and a great deal of jest. Lame Deer named Sitting Bull, Black Elk, and the famed Crazy Horse as bearers of these secret *winkte* names. The names could make one famous. "Well, this man-woman told me that in the old days the *winktes* used to call each other sisters and had a special hill where they were buried. I asked him when he died, when he went south, what he would be in the spirit land, a man or a woman. He told me he would be both. It was a long interview, lasting through two bottles of wine" (1972:150).

A melancholy permeates John Lame Deer's words, even within the trace of humor, a nostalgic bending toward the traditional past, the glory, the freedom that can never again be known by the Indian and an honor bestowed upon a *winkte*.

Recently a middle-aged Navajo berdache said that he was not accepted in the off-reservation world, but while living with his people, the traditional Navajos, he is paid respect because it was the berdache who kept the men and women, the people, together as a unit, a tribe. He may have been referring to the Turquoise Boy, the hermaphrodite who helped bring the Navajos into the fifth and present world. This man, an off-reservation transvestite who is no longer revered in ceremony, insists that Indians condone homosexuality. Other young Indians, members of Gay American Indians, have organized in San Francisco to fight the current ignorance and abuse directed toward them by their own reservation brothers and sisters. Perhaps when Indians have once again regained their old cultures, languages, and ceremonies, the berdache not only will be respected but will find a place in his chosen society. The current taboos against his nature will then have changed sufficiently so that he may make a contribution to and function once more in that reorganized culture.

MIDNIGHT SUN
ANISHNAWBE

SEX/GENDER SYSTEMS IN NATIVE NORTH AMERICA

INTRODUCTION

The four-hundred-year history of ethnographic documentation on Native American people has been selective. This selectivity is most pronounced in the literature dealing with sex and gender relations, especially where these deviated from the bipolar European norm of the heterosexual "man" and "woman" and contradicted the European patriarchal world view. As a result, the existence of different gender systems among native people has often been presented from a narrow perspective.

Today it is commonplace to describe gender and sexuality as culturally constructed rather than biologically or naturally determined. To support this view, many theorists have used cross-cultural examples to show different patterns of organizing sexual behavior and gender characteristics, often in an attempt to compare these patterns with those found in western industrialized society. The point of such comparisons is to demonstrate that the manner in which gender and sexuality are organized and patterned in contemporary western society is a cultural phenomenon, rather than the result of immutable biological forces.

Such an approach, however, tends to isolate one set of cultural phenomena—those specifically relating to gender and sexuality—from their wider social and economic contexts. So, for example, Evelyn Blackwood, in looking at precolonial cross-gender females of various Native American groups, discusses cross-dressing and

I would like to acknowledge the assistance of Jackie Crawford, who collaborated on an earlier version of this chapter in 1985, and Will Roscoe, for extensive editorial suggestions and continuing encouragement.

lesbian sexual behavior in terms of "Native American society" and "Native ideology" (Blackwood 1984). This ignores significant differences in subsistence patterns, kinship, and social organization among the groups she describes, and dislocates such phenomena from their social, economic, and political contexts. Blackwood and others focus on the cultural construction of gender and sexuality as an ideological process. While such an approach is valuable, it raises many questions.

There is a tendency, for example, to see homosexuality or lesbianism as ahistorical, universal entities occurring at different times and in different cultures. But this is incompatible with a view of sexuality as culturally constructed, if by "construction" we mean the socially ordained patterns for meeting individual biological sexual needs that cultures establish. Yet there is a tendency to conflate the "universal" or "essentialist" and the "social constructionist" approaches and to use contemporary western concepts of sex, gender, and sexuality as standards for comparing all other cultures.

Cross-cultural material is often used to support claims about contemporary western homosexuality. In a discussion of her own work, Mary McIntosh speaks of "starting with a very schematic definition of what the modern homosexual role was and going round looking for it in history" (McIntosh 1981:47). As she suggests, this approach is problematic for two reasons, the most obvious being that quite different cultural phenomena are compared when they are viewed in terms of the theorist's starting point. Second, this approach isolates cultural characteristics from their contexts. For example, in the McIntosh discussion Jeffrey Weeks asks, "Why should one even begin to contemplate the notion that the berdache has anything at all to do with homosexuality in our terms?" (Weeks in Plummer 1981:48). Because he locates the berdache in a social and economic context fundamentally different from contemporary western society, Weeks concludes that viewing the berdache as a variation of the homosexual role is inaccurate and misleading.

Social, and specifically sexual, life is embedded in the economic organization of society—an organization that gives rise to a variety of cultural forms. The cultural construction of gender and sexuality must be seen in terms of the sexual division of labor, subsistence patterns, social relations, and male-female relations. Within this context, ideology is not an arbitrary, discrete force—rather, it serves to reproduce and perpetuate social forms, behaviors, and individuals suitable to a particular mode of production.

The relationships between the economic, ideological, and sex/gender systems of Native American societies can best be seen in the changes brought about by colonialization. Fundamental changes in economic patterns disrupted many aspects of native social life, including gender and sexuality. In this chapter, ethnographic and historical material will be used to show how these changes led to alterations in the construction of native sexuality and gender.

I follow Gayle Rubin's definition of the sex/gender system as "a set of arrangements by which a society transforms biological sexuality into products of human activity, and in which these transformed sexual needs are satisfied" (Rubin 1975:159). While I give some attention to these "arrangements" that sanction patterns of gender and sexuality, the relation of these to a society's economic organization is my primary focus. The role of the Navajo *nadle,* for example, emerges from a horticultural economy that provided women a high degree of autonomy, along with kinship and residence patterns that allowed same-sex communal activities. The importance of this role to the Navajo economy will be stressed and will be the focus for examining Navajo ideology as it relates to cross-dressing, cross-gender roles, and same-sex sexuality.

One of the most frequently used terms in the literature is *berdache,* derived from a Persian word meaning "kept boy" or "male prostitute" and first applied by French explorers to designate "passive" partners in homosexual relationships between Native American males (Angelino and Shedd 1955:121). This is complicated, however, by the fact that many individuals labeled berdaches also engaged in cross-dressing and cross-gender behavior. Most ethnographers have interpreted this behavior as indicating the assumption of another gender role. The berdache, therefore, has been defined as a person of one sex who assumed the gender role of the other sex, cross-dressing as part of the assumed role. At the same time, individuals with physically ambiguous genitalia—hermaphrodites or intersexes—were often termed berdaches, as well—not because they assumed the gender role of either sex but because they combined roles to create a third gender.

The distinction between gender role and sexual preference is important, in particular when using the terms *cross-dressing, cross-gender,* and *lesbian* or *homosexual* behavior. These terms are in themselves awkward and ethnocentric. If a culture's sex/gender system makes it possible for a biological female to become a social man, then "he" is not engaging in "cross-dressing" when dressing as a male, or in "cross-gender" behavior by assuming the culturally defined male role. Neither is "he" engaging in lesbian behavior by having sexual relations with women. Because he is a socially recognized man, such relations would be defined as "normal."

All these terms relate to one another and to the mode of production in specific ways, and they must be distinguished. I use "cross-dressing" to refer to male or female transvestism; "cross-gender behavior" to the assumption of the role of the other sex; and "homosexual" or "lesbian" to refer to the identity of those engaging in patterned same-sex sexual behavior. This latter definition distinguishes between behavior and identity and also separates male homosexuality from lesbianism. This is important, not only because homosexuality and lesbianism are constructed and perceived differently, but also because they will be discussed as specific aspects of sexuality.

Many ethnographers have recorded and interpreted material on sex and gender using a paradigm specific to their own cultural viewpoint, biased by androcentricism and heterosexism, while disregarding material conditions such as the mode of production, kinship, residence patterns, indigenous concepts of power, myth, marital relations, and socially appropriate behavior. Their ethnographies are often frustratingly inadequate and must be read with caution.

Upon discovering the existence of cross-gender individuals, George Catlin, an early ethnographer, remarked, "This is one of the most unaccountable and disgusting customs that I have ever met in the Indian country" (Catlin 1973b:215). Indeed, the impact of colonization on native lifestyles and ideologies has forced native constructions of gender and sexuality to conform to western types. As the anthropologist Alfred Kroeber noted: "While the [cross-gender] institution was in full bloom, the Caucasian attitude was one of repugnance and condemnation. This attitude . . . made subsequent personality inquiry difficult, the later berdaches leading repressed or disguised lives" (Kroeber 1940:209).

While many sex/gender systems are no longer in existence, historical source material can be reanalyzed and reinterpreted using another paradigm—that of the cultural construction of sex, gender, and sexuality.

THE ETHNOGRAPHIC MATERIAL

I will use three major case studies to illustrate various native concepts of homosexuality, lesbianism, cross-dressing, and gender roles among the Mojave, Navajo, and Peigan (Northern Blackfeet) tribes. These cultures represent three types of descent patterns, subsistence activities, forms of warfare, and geographic location. All three studies were compiled some fifty years ago (from 1935 to 1941). Although informants stated that cross-dressers were prevalent in previous times, by the turn of the century initiation ceremonies were no longer being performed and attitudes toward sex and gender had been influenced by European Christian values.

The Mojave

The Mojave are a southwestern American tribe who occupy regions of Arizona, California, and Nevada along the Colorado River. In the late seventeenth century they numbered three thousand and subsisted on small-scale agriculture, supplemented by gathering, hunting, and fishing (Dutton 1976:27). This subsistence strategy, combined with Mojave kinship, marriage, and residence patterns, allowed for relatively egalitarian male-female relations. However, a developed system of warfare and an emphasis on male values such as bravery and skills in battle contributed to an ideological masculinization of Mojave society.

In the mid-1930s George Devereux, a Freudian anthropologist, completed several studies on sexuality and berdache roles in Mojave society. To date, this remains the most comprehensive ethnography on a North American sex/gender system. Devereux does not mention the existence of hermaphrodites, focusing instead on homosexual and lesbian cross-dressers termed *alyha* (male) and *hwame* (female). Not all homosexual or lesbian behavior entailed assumption of the *alyha* or *hwame* roles, however. Those who were involved in marital or sexual relationships with *alyha* or *hwame*, for example, retained the gender identity associated with their biological sex. In other words, Mojave cross-gender categories were distinct from their categories of man and woman.

The assumption of the *alyha* and *hwame* roles was predestined by dreams. If a pregnant woman dreamed of masculine implements, such as arrow-feathers, her female child could become a *hwame*. If she dreamed of objects associated with women, her male child could grow up to become an *alyha*. Throughout the child's initial years, these tendencies remained latent, but during the period when children were initiated into their appropriate gender roles, cross-gender behavior emerged. A boy wore female clothes and associated with girls. A girl behaved in the opposite manner, refusing to perform female tasks (Devereux 1937 :501–502). Thus gender roles and sexual identities were defined by the age of ten to twelve years. There are few reports of people older than this beginning to engage in cross-dressing. It can be seen, then, that these cross-gender roles were cultural constructs allowing the socialization of these children to a sanctioned sexual and gender identity.

Mojave cross-gender identities allowed individuals to assume some aspects of both masculine and feminine gender roles so that, for instance, an *alyha* could engage in traditionally feminine activities, such as pottery and craftwork, as well as some masculine activities. In this way, the *alyha* avoided some aspects of the masculine role, while engaging in certain production activities related to both gender roles, gaining access to additional economic opportunity and the potential for accruing wealth. The same is true for the *hwame*: these cross-gender women were always regarded as excelling in their endeavors and succeeding economically.

The Mojave believed that cross-gender individuals, especially *hwames,* were lucky in gambling and could become powerful shamans, while shamans and chiefs often married *alyhas.* The *alyha* was reported to be a valuable wife and had no difficulty in obtaining a husband because the Mojave were adventuresome and had an accepting attitude toward sexuality. The *alyha* wife provided a high degree of economic comfort and prestige through "her" ability to excel in productive activities.

Alyhas and *hwames* not only adopted the characteristics of the other gender—they fictively conformed to the biological sex characteristics of their assumed genders. For instance, it was reported that when an *alyha* found a potential husband he imitated menstruation by scratching his legs until they bled. As all women did, he submitted to puberty and menstruation observances. The *alyha* would also create a hypothetical pregnancy during which he would stop menstruating and observe customary pregnancy taboos, obeying them even more strictly than women (Devereux 1937:512).

"Normal" women did not discuss pregnancy publicly, but *alyhas* boasted about it. Stuffing clothes under their skirts, they indicated advanced pregnancy. When delivery time drew near, they ate a mixture of mesquite beans that caused constipation and severe abdominal cramps, and they feigned labor pains. They gave birth alone, away from the village, and pretended that stillbirth had occurred. They observed mourning rituals for the lost child, cutting their own and their husbands' hair. An *alyha*'s husband was often ridiculed for his wife's actions and for his childless marriage.

Divorcing an *alyha* was not easy. They resisted and were able to beat up their husbands. If a husband used barrenness as grounds for leaving, the *alyha* faked pregnancy again. *Alyhas* were not teased, because it was thought they could not help themselves. But their husbands bore the brunt of ridicule, and this was believed to contribute to unstable marriages (Devereux 1937:514).

Hwames found wives at dances and through visiting—they could not risk normal courtship for fear of the girl's parents' objections. The Mojave believed that intercourse with a pregnant woman could change the paternity of a child, so if a *hwame* seduced a pregnant woman, "he" was entitled to claim paternity and take care of the infant. When fulfilling the role of husband, *hwame* women did not observe their own menstruation taboos, but those of their wives. At social gatherings, *hwames* sat with the men and discussed their sexual practices and their wives' genitals. It was general opinion that "no one ever expected a *hwame* to behave herself" (Devereux 1937:515).

Mojave cross-gender roles were ideologically sanctioned in various ways. Their creation story includes the role of the berdache. "Ever since the world began at *Avi-kwame,* it is said that there have been transvestites," and "from the beginning of the world, it was meant that there should be homosexuals." The fact that cross-gender individuals were often shamans or married to shamans or chiefs suggests not only cultural acceptance, but an association with status and prestige, as well. This may be due to their value in production, because they could combine elements of both masculine and feminine economic spheres.

By the time of Devereux's work, however, Mojave culture had been disrupted by centuries of colonization. The traditional Mojave economic base was no longer viable, having been replaced by wage labor within a capitalist economy. As a result, social organization underwent massive change and the traditional sex/gender system was radically altered.

While cross-gender roles continued to exist at the time of Devereux's study, their form was markedly different and cultural attitudes toward them had become disparaging, in conformity with western attitudes. The Mojave had begun to view such individuals as "somewhat crazy," and families were ashamed to have one as a member (Devereux 1937:502).

Similarly, *hwame* were said to be "lewd women who throw away their housekeeping implements and run wild" (Devereux 1937:503). Mojave women were less willing to marry a *hwame* because of the fear of being shunned later by men, the lack of physical protection from rape, and the inability to have children. In precolonial times, marriage, divorce, and the adoption of children were organized differently so that these would not have been concerns of the wives of *hwames*. But changes in the nature of Mojave production had required changes in family organization. Mojave women became economically dependent on men and heterosexual marriage. The *alyha* and *hwame* roles were no longer economically viable, and this contributed to the decline of these identities.

The Navajo

The Navajo, a tribe numbering more than 125,000 today, occupy areas of Arizona, Colorado, and New Mexico. During the precontact period, they were primarily foragers and small game hunters. In the eighteenth century, as a result of European influence, they turned to horticulture and sheep herding as their main subsistence strategy (Driver 1969:60). The high degree of participation of Navajo women in production and the economic sphere was related to several aspects of Navajo life. The absence of a developed system of warfare and any form of social stratification, and the practice of matrilocal residence, matrilineal descent, and serial monogamy, all contributed to relatively egalitarian male-female relations.

Among the Navajo, the term for both hermaphrodites and cross-dressers was *nadle,* which means "he changes" (Young and Morgan 1980:525). Hermaphrodites were distinguished as "real *nadle*" and cross-dressers as "pretend *nadle*"—yet both were accorded the same status. The Navajo recognized three distinct categories of sex and gender: male, female, and *nadle.* Hermaphrodites were said to have preferred women's clothing and male sexual partners and never to have married. "Pretend *nadles*" chose the apparel, behavior, and sexual partners of either sex (Hill 1935:275) and were referred to by male or female kinship terms according to the clothes they wore (Reichard 1969:150). Male *nadles* usually assumed a feminine gender role and identified with other women at dances and social occasions. They had the legal status of women, which was higher than that of men (Hill 1935:275).

At the time of Hill's report, male and female cross-dressers were of equal number. Their unique behavior was said to have manifested itself early in childhood, when the individual began to assume the gender role of the other sex. *Nadles* undertook the duties of both sexes and excelled in their dual economic roles. They supervised women's work, undertook domestic duties, raised sheep, wove, and made pottery and baskets. As well, they were accomplished midwives, healers, and chanters. The *nadle*'s ability to fulfill and excel at the occupational roles of both sexes must have contributed to the favorable attitude toward them in Navajo religious ideology. Their cultural role is well substantiated in myths that served, in general, to validate and reinforce the sex/gender system.

Because they were believed to have been given charge of wealth since the beginning of time, a family with a *nadle* was considered fortunate and assured of wealth and success (Hill 1935:274). This philosophy is expressed in such statements as "I think when all the *nadle* are gone, that it will be the end of the Navajo," and "If there were no *nadle*, the country would change" (Hill 1935:274). These attitudes reflected the right of *nadles* to control and dispose of property and their ability to accumulate wealth because of their access to various economic endeavors.

The Navajo sanctioned their cross-gender role by according such individuals an elevated political and social status. As a result, the *nadle* was in a position distinct from either sex, with a greater opportunity for personal and material gain than ordinary individuals.

The Peigan

The last ethnography is from a Canadian plains culture, the northern Peigan, who, together with the Blackfeet and Blood tribes, formed the Blackfeet Confederacy. With the introduction of the horse, the Peigan hunting-and-gathering mode of subsistence gave way to the classic buffalo-hunting culture, which was accompanied by a well-developed system of warfare, the practice of polygyny, social stratification, patrilocal residence, and a bilateral descent pattern (Driver 1969:57,230,260).

The Blackfeet placed a premium on male values and ideals of bravery, success in warfare, wealth, and generosity. They accorded social value to men and channeled prestige to them via patrilocal residence, bride price, a sexual double standard, age grades, and exclusive participation in tribal government (Lewis 1941:173–75; Martin and Voorhies 1975:101). The ownership, manipulation, and distribution of property were emphasized, and there was a marked contrast between rich and poor. Material objects like horses became an important commodity to index social status.

Despite the elevation of male values, a unique role for women did emerge, distinct from the *nadle* and *hwame* roles, called the *ninauposkitzipxpe,* or "manly-hearted woman." While not a berdache role, this position represented a behavior pattern in striking contrast to the Peigan feminine ideal of submission, loyalty, and fidelity (Lewis 1941:173; Martin and Voorhies 1975:101).

While deviating from the general Peigan ideal of women, manly-hearted women did conform on a broader level to the feminine social role. They were not lesbians or cross-dressers, but a small group of married individuals possessing certain traits considered masculine by the Peigan, such as aggression, independence, ambition, boldness, and confident sexuality. Not just any women who behaved this way would be entitled to the term of manly-hearted, however, but only those of a certain status who manifested these characteristics in particular social settings (Lewis 1941:175).

Manly-hearted women were easily distinguished by their interest in and ownership of property, nonconformist behavior, superior dress, and active participation in religious affairs. Because manly-hearts took an unusual interest in appearance, they (and their husbands) wore the best clothes on public occasions. Unlike most Peigan men who were possessive, the husbands of manly-hearts took pride in the public admiration of their wives. These women talked freely to men and did not hesitate to make speeches, express opinions, or choose partners at a dance. They were by no means shy and were known to speak loudly and use profane language. The only woman reported to have sung mens' songs in ceremonies was a manly-hearted woman (Lewis 1941:180–81). They were more independent, self-assured, and aggressive than other women and more respected by men.

Because manly-hearts conducted business affairs without interference, it was general opinion that they dominated their husbands and controlled their family's economic affairs. These men had to consult their wives and obtain permission regarding business transactions. The Peigan said, "It's easy to spot a manly-hearted woman: the husband simply has nothing to say" (Lewis 1941:181).

The Peigan made a clear distinction between real manly-hearts (traditional) and would-be manly-hearts (contemporary upstarts), based on specific qualifications. Property ownership was the main prerequisite. Manly-hearted women were able to accumulate property through inheritance, their own endeavors, and gifts. They excelled in both masculine and feminine occupations and were considered efficient, ambitious, and hard-working. Their ability to create surplus enabled them to amass capital and purchase horses and other material possessions. As widows and divorcées, they could remain self-sufficient and independent, and thus make a free choice as to whether and whom to marry (Lewis 1941:178).

Lewis's study of fourteen manly-hearted women on the Brockett Reserve in Alberta revealed that they owned more property than all other women on the reserve combined (Lewis 1941:178). This was, in part, due to the fact that manly-hearts had a different attitude toward marital property relations and insisted that their property was strictly their own. Many Peigan men owed their wealth and community status to the hard work and perseverance of their manly-hearted wives, whose economic success was the only justification allowed by men for a woman to dominate her husband (Lewis 1941:178).

The second requirement was maturity. There were progressively more manly-hearts in older age categories. The majority were over fifty. Several reasons might explain this phenomenon. It often took considerable time to accumulate the wealth and prestige needed to be considered manly-hearted. Older women might have been married more than once and have inherited substantial property. Finally, it took time to cultivate the confidence of the community needed to assume the role (Lewis 1941:176).

The Peigan believe that "a poor woman would not have the nerve to do things that are considered manly-hearted" (Lewis 1941:177).

Although these women shared the same status, all did not go through the same stages of development. Often the role has been associated with *minipoka* (favored children), who enjoyed unusual opportunities and access to wealth, property, and participation in religious activities. From early childhood, they were set apart from others. They were less shy, more dominating, and had an air of importance. Forty percent of the manly-hearts in Lewis's study had also been *minipoka* (Lewis 1941:185).

Lewis interprets the high proportion of favored children among manly-hearts as a result of the *minipokas'* inability to fulfill the feminine role and "adapt themselves to changes sometimes brutally extreme" (Lewis 1941:186). The great age difference between girls and their husbands led to difficulties and a reversal of the conditions under which some girls grew up. Some women, married as young as the age of nine, faced heavy work demands and the possibility of physical abuse from their husbands. (Peigan parents did not hit their children, however.) "[The *minipokas*] were no longer attended but had to attend, they were no longer without responsibilities but had many duties, they no longer went unpunished but were at the mercy of their husbands" (Lewis 1941:186).

Even though manly-hearted women were successful and respected, Peigans felt ambiguous about them. Other women considered them immodest and dreaded the thought of their daughters becoming one. Yet, at the same time, they were admired and envied for their courage, skill, and freedom.

Manly-heart status enabled some women to escape the restrictions of the feminine gender role within a heavily male-dominated society. The manly-heart role was narrowly defined but allowed some Peigan women a culturally sanctioned manner in which to achieve a degree of independence. It is interesting that only women of a particular age and status could assume this role and also that it was associated only with gender status and not cross-dressing or lesbianism.

The kinship, residence, and overall subsistence patterns of Peigan society involved heterosexual household units within a patriarchal culture. The feminine gender role involved little status or power and little scope for economic independence. The manly-hearted role allowed certain women to achieve relatively high social and economic status, but in male-defined terms. Men married to manly-hearts benefited from their wives' wealth and success, and it is significant that only married women could assume the role. It is also interesting to note that while upstarts displayed similar personal characteristics, they lacked the means and resources of manly-hearted women and were not defined as manly-hearts.

The role can be seen as a cultural strategy to preserve the social and economic stratification of the sexes in Peigan society, allowing certain women access to male power and resources in male-defined ways. The manly-heart identity preserved the male-dominant structure of society by allowing a few specific women a narrowly defined gender role in which to enact nonfeminine characteristics, while continuing to be seen as women and while remaining married.

DISCUSSION

Sex/gender systems must be seen in historical materialist terms. They are shaped, in part, to meet economic interests and reinforced and validated by the dominant ideology, including religion and normative rules. Lack of information regarding indigenous ideologies makes analysis difficult, but certain hypotheses may be made by attempting to situate native sex/gender systems in contexts specific to their societies.

Here I delineate differences between the three cultures described in an attempt to explain some of the factors that contributed to the construction of their sex/gender systems. This is followed by a general discussion of native constructions of gender and sexuality.

The Navajo were engaged in a horticultural subsistence strategy, a mode of production in which women were heavily involved. In this society, women's economic participation contributed to the development of matrilineal descent and matrilocal residence. Both were associated with women's high degree of autonomy and relatively egalitarian relations between men and women. Also, Navajo attitudes toward marriage, divorce, the adoption of children, and sexuality were tolerant by western standards. Navajo women were relatively independent of the control of men, owned and controlled their own produce, and had the support of other women based on the kinship network—all factors that shaped and are reflected in the Navajo sex/gender system. Because women were not required to fulfill functions defined by men and because the sexual division of labor was defined so as to allow the possibility of mixing or combining male and female work roles, the cross-gender role was a viable option for both men and women.

The Mojave also depended on horticulture, yet women's participation in economic production was counterbalanced by factors that did not affect their Navajo neighbors. Due to the existence of intertribal conflict, the Mojave had a well-developed system of warfare and emphasized male values and pursuits. This had an adverse effect on cross-gender individuals, who were considered less than ideal men and women.

Rigid construction of gender roles may explain why cross-gender individuals not only assumed the dress and mannerisms associated with the other sex but also feigned biological sex characteristics. For instance, female *hwames* did not observe their own menstruation taboos, while male *alyhas* faked menstruation and pregnancy, and neither referred to their real genitalia. It is possible that in the strict sex/gender system of the Mojave, with its clear separation of activities related to male and female sex roles, such close adherence to biological sex characteristics was a necessary and logical part of their cross-gender roles.

Peigan culture was male-dominated and typical of the classical buffalo-hunting period. Although the Peigan allowed for some gender variation, female sexuality was rigidly constrained to fit the ideal of monogamous heterosexual marriage. There was a discrepancy between women's economic and religious roles and the established standard of female behavior, which required women to relegate themselves to the background of life (Lewis 1941:187). Although men were accorded greater social esteem, patterns of production and allocation did favor some women. Hence, manly-hearted women were able to take advantage of unique opportunities and to compete and succeed with men on their own terms.

In a male-dominated society, the manly-hearted role was one of the few available routes for Peigan women to successfully match a man in prestige. Through their industrious work and capabilities, these women were able to command the resources necessary to masculinize their status. But they were required to achieve social distinction on male terms, which ultimately reinforced Peigan ideals of appropriate sexuality.

There are numerous perspectives on the causality of cross-dressing behavior, homosexuality, and lesbianism, including theories that suggest they are a result of early socialization, hereditary defects, genetic variations, or lack of heterosexual outlets (Bullough 1979:10–16; Whitehead 1981:83). These hypotheses represent ideological perspectives that must be seen as peculiar to the western European tradition.

Some ethnographers have hypothesized that cross-gender roles were a niche for homosexuals in "drag" (Devereux 1937:320) or an escape from the ideal gender roles of some societies (Driver 1969:442). But analysis of the literature reveals that occupation, dress, and demeanor were more important than sexual preference. Homosexual relations were accepted without the requirement to cross-dress and were not considered the basis of sexual orientations. Alone, homosexuality or lesbianism was not enough to provoke gender reclassification, which was based on social identity and not sexuality.

As this review has shown, sex/gender systems and cross-gender roles are related to the means of production of the society in which they occur. By studying cross-gender roles among the Mojave, Navajo, and Peigan in terms of their relationship to the mode of production, we have seen how, when production changes, gender roles and cross-gender roles change, as well. The advantage of this approach is that it allows us to see a society's social organization—and its berdache or cross-gender roles—in terms of that society, without filtering data through cultural perceptions alien to the societies we study.

WILL ROSCOE

STRANGE COUNTRY THIS: IMAGES OF BERDACHES AND WARRIOR WOMEN

FIRST ENCOUNTER

TIMUCUA

"Without the succour of that Indian Hermaphrodite . . ."

The European voyagers to America did not have words in their own languages for referring to berdaches. In the 1500s the French and Spanish competing for control of Florida used terms like *hermaphrodite* (French and English), *garçon effemines* (French), and *hombres mariones impotentes* (Spanish).

All these different terms created confusion. But at least one report makes it clear that they refer to the same role we now call berdache. In 1722 François Coreal described "effeminate youths" *(garçon effemines)* he had observed in Florida, noting that "they are confused with the *Hermaphrodites* which they say are found in quantity in the country of the Floridians. I believe that these *Hermaphrodites* are none other than the effeminate youths" (34).

Coreal had probably visited the Timucuans. These Florida Indians were farmers and villagers. They had a complex society, organized into castes. The Europeans referred to their chiefs as kings.

Rene Goulaine de Laudonniere arrived in Florida in 1564 to build a fort for the French. At one point he attempted a march through the dense Florida woodlands on a hot day. His party was nearly exhausted and nowhere in sight of its destination when "an Hermaphrodite . . . came before us with a great vessell full of cleere fountaine water." According to Laudonniere, "without the succour of that Indian Hermaphrodite" his party would have

First Encounter (Timucua).
Engraving by Theodor De Bry (1590),
Courtesy Rare Books and Manuscripts Division, New York Public Library, Astor, Lenox, and Tilden Foundations.

been unable to proceed, but, "being therefore refreshed by this meane, wee gathered our spirits together, and marching with a cheerefull courage, wee came to the place which wee had chosen to make our habitation in" (1904:16).

According to Jacques Le Moyne—the artist who painted the picture on which this engraving is based—"hermaphrodites," because of their strength, carried provisions when the men went to war. They buried the dead, and, in cases of injury or illness, they would "take the sick on their shoulders to places selected for the purpose and feed and care for them until they are well again"

(1965:69). While Timucuan berdaches wore at least some female attire, they could be distinguished from both men and women by the color of the feathers they wore in their hair (Coreal 1722:34).

The sexuality of Timucuan berdaches is also well attested. Native Floridians allowed marriages between men (Torquemada 1943:427), and berdaches participated in "sodomy"—an act to which the males in general were "strongly inclined" (Coreal 1722:33). Because of these cultural traits, Francisco de Pareja, a Franciscan missionary sent to Florida in 1595, routinely asked his male and female converts to confess homosexual acts (1976:287).

Timucuan culture did not survive its exposure to European "civilization." When the Spanish finally left Florida in 1763, the eighty-three Christianized Timucuans still alive went with them.

CALIFORNIA SHAMAN

TOLOWA

"He never came back . . ."

Coming from a sexually repressed culture with little tolerance for individual differences, the Spanish Franciscan fathers who founded the California missions were dumbfounded when they first encountered berdaches:

> Among the gentile women . . . there was one who . . . had all the appearances of a woman, but judging by the face and the absence of breasts, though old enough for that, they concluded he must be a man. . . . Taking off his aprons they found that he was more ashamed than if he really had been a woman. They kept him there three days, making him sweep the plaza, but giving him plenty to eat. But he remained very cast down and ashamed. After he had been warned that it was not right for him to go about dressed as a woman and much less thrust himself in with them, as it was presumed that he was sinning with them, they let him go. He immediately left the Mission and never came back to it, but from the converts it was learned that he was still in the villages of the gen-

tiles and going about as before, dressed as a woman. (Palou 1913: 215)

The fathers found berdaches at several missions and suppressed the role whenever they could. In the end, however, all mission Indians suffered a similar fate. Disease, demoralization, and poor conditions resulted in a drastic reduction in population and the loss of tribal culture.

Thirty-four California tribes have been reported to have berdaches. Fortunately, not all experienced the devastation of missionization.

The Tolowa, for example, an Athabaskan-speaking tribe on the northern California coast, had little contact with whites until the 1820s. At that time they lived in eight villages near Crescent City. They hunted, fished, and gathered wild foods. Tolowa women were expert basket-makers.

Among the Tolowa, shamans cured both physical and spiritual ills. According to anthropologist Richard A. Gould, shamans "were mainly women or transvestite males" (1978:134). They danced and entered trances, and then sucked out of the patient or vomited up the foreign object believed to be the cause of the illness.

This 1910 photograph shows a Tolowa berdache shaman, or *minhushre*. Gould describes the figure: "In his nose he wears a horizontal bone noseplug and vertical dentalium shell beads; both denote his wealth. Hat, collar-necklace of trade beads and coins, and dance apron are all women's apparel. The apron is fringed with thimble tinklers. . . . The collar-necklace is made of perforated coins" (1978:131).

In California, berdaches were not always shamans, however. Among the Mono and Yokuts tribes, they had a different role: preparing the dead for burial. And, in many tribes, berdaches specialized in crafts, such as basketry, rather than religious roles.

California Shaman (Tolowa).

Courtesy National Anthropological Archives, Smithsonian Institution, neg. no. 81–2130.

DANCE TO THE BERDASHE

SAUK AND FOX

"Extraordinary privileges . . ."

The series of portraits and scenes painted by George Catlin in the 1830s provide a valuable record of plains Indian life before the reservation period. Catlin witnessed the ceremony depicted in this painting while visiting the Sauk and Fox Indians. His hosts held a dance in honor of the tribe's berdaches—the *i-coo-coo-a,* or *aya'kwa* (Michelson 1925:256).

The *aya'kwa* both appalled and fascinated Catlin. His description swings from condemnation to hints of more positive Sauk and Fox attitudes:

> The *"Berdashe"* . . . is a man dressed in woman's clothes, as he is known to be all his life, and for extraordinary privileges which he is known to possess, he is driven to the most servile and degrading duties, which he is not allowed to escape; and he being the only one of the tribe submitting to this disgraceful degradation, is looked upon as *medicine* and sacred, and a feast is given to him annually. (1973b:214–15)

According to Catlin, the men who participated in the dance had to make a public "boast." What this was Catlin does not say, except that "few in the tribe . . . have legitimately gained this singular privilege" (1973b:215).

Some sixty years later Fox berdaches were described again, by folklorist Mary Owen.

> They were considered "good medicine" for the tribe; and the women insured a share of it by leaving cooked food and bundles of wood at their doors, when no one was observing. Once a year, a feast and dance was given them, at which some of the young men of the common people took them by the hands, danced with them, insulted them by pretended love-making, and finally gave them presents of old clothes begged or bought from the squaws. While the dance was

Dance to the Berdashe (Sauk and Fox).
Painting by George Catlin (1835–1837),
Courtesy National Museum of American Art, Smithsonian Institution.

> in progress, the on-lookers of both sexes kept up a continual clapping, and shouted "I-coo-coo-ah" and "Hoo-hoo-henow-chee-chee." (1902:54–55)

Apparently the men who participated in the dance had all been sexual partners of the *aya'kwa.* In typical Indian fashion, this was the source of much joking. While the men teased the berdache, the berdache, no doubt, teased the men in return, using the intimate knowledge he had gained of them during their sexual encounters. (Dakota, or Sioux, *winkte* were also famous for this sort of teasing.)

According to Owen, the traditional *aya'kwa* role and the "Dance to the Berdache" lapsed around 1900.

WE'WHA

ZUNI

"A notable character . . ."

By any standards, the Zuni berdache (or *lhamana)* We'wha (1849–1896) was an important member of his tribe. He has been described as "the strongest character and the most intelligent of the Zuni tribe" (Stevenson 1904:20); "one of the most noted and prominent" members of the tribe (James n.d.); and "that man of enormous strength who lived a woman's daily life in woman's dress, but remained a power in his Pueblo's gravest councils" (Bunker 1956:99–100). Zunis today still recall stories about We'wha.

We'wha was accomplished in both weaving and pottery. He was well versed in sacred and secular lore, and he participated in male religious activities. He managed the large household of his adopted family, and he became one of the first Zunis to earn cash, washing clothes for whites and selling his weaving and pottery (Stevenson 1904).

We'wha became friends with Matilda Coxe Stevenson, an anthropologist who published a long report on the Zunis in 1904. Stevenson described We'wha as "perhaps the tallest person in Zuni; certainly the strongest." Even so, for several years Stevenson believed We'wha was a woman, and she insisted on using the female pronoun when writing about him (1904:310).

In 1886 We'wha spent six months in the national capital as Stevenson's guest. Washington society accepted him as a Zuni "priestess," "princess," and "maiden." He participated in a theatrical charity event sponsored by society women, and he called on Speaker of the House John Carlisle and President Grover Cleveland. He demonstrated weaving at the Smithsonian and helped Stevenson document Zuni culture.

We'wha (Zuni).

Courtesy National Anthropological Archives, Smithsonian Institution, neg. no. 2235-a.

According to the writer Edmund Wilson, when We'wha returned to Zuni, "He assured his compatriots that the white women were mostly frauds, for he had seen them, in the ladies' rooms, taking out their false teeth and the 'rats' from their hair" (1956:20).

One of the most moving passages in Stevenson's report is her account of We'wha's death in 1896. Stevenson joined the family gathered around We'wha to hear his final words:

> We'wha asked the writer to come close and in a feeble voice she said, in English: "Mother, I am going to the other world. I will tell the gods of you and Captain Stevenson. I will tell them of Captain Carlisle, the great seed priest, and his wife, whom I love. They are my friends. Tell them good-by. Tell all my friends in Washington good-by. Tell President Cleveland, my friend, good-by. Mother, love all my people; protect them; they are your children; you are their mother." . . . She leaned forward with the [prayersticks] tightly clasped, and as the setting sun lighted up the western windows, darkness and desolation entered the hearts of the mourners, for We'wha was dead. (Stevenson 1904:311–12)

To symbolize his berdache status—an individual who bridged the roles of men and women—We'wha was buried in a woman's dress, with a pair of man's pants slipped on beneath.

MOJARO

ACOMA

"The best potters of Acoma . . ."

The Keres of Acoma and nearby Laguna speak a language distinct from the Zunis', but they share many cultural forms. Like the Zunis, they impersonate their gods in the form of masked dancers, called kachinas. One set of Acoma-Laguna kachinas portray supernatural men-women who dance in commemoration of mythological events (see "The Battle of the Sto-ro-ka and the Ka-tsina," p. 86). They wear women's dresses with men's pants beneath.

Mojaro (Acoma).
Courtesy National Anthropological Archives, Smithsonian Institution, neg. no. 74–662.

This photograph was taken in 1900 by Sumner W. Matteson. The note with it reads: "The *mojaro,* or 'man in woman's clothing,' of Acoma with sister on left and niece on his right. They are the finest potters of Acoma. This man has elected to dress like a woman and do woman's work rather than fight. He is far more particular of dress than the women" (Casagrande and Bourns 1983:229).

Laguna also had a famous berdache potter in the late nineteenth century, identified by Jonathan Batkin as Arroh-ah-och (Bunzel 1972:57; pers., comm., 3 March 1987).

One of the earliest accounts of a berdache among the Pueblos is by William A. Hammond, an army doctor who examined an Acoma berdache in the 1850s. According to Hammond, berdaches were called *mujerados,* a Spanish word (Hammond 1887:163–67). Other versions include *amugereados, mohara,* and *mujeringo.* The Keresan word for berdaches is *kokwima* (Parsons 1923:166).

FINDS THEM AND KILLS THEM

CROW

"Distinguished by his bravery . . ."

Finds Them and Kills Them, or Osh-Tisch, (1854–1929) was one of the last traditional Crow berdaches or *boté.* He died after a long and colorful life spanning the last years of armed conflict and the first years of reservation life.

Ethnohistorian Walter L. Williams visited the Crow reservation of Montana in 1982 and found elders who remembered Finds Them and Kills Them. According to Joe Medicine Crow: "Osh-Tisch . . . got his name in 1876, when he turned warrior for that one day. He put on men's clothes and attacked a Lakota party in the Battle of the Rosebud, and was distinguished by his bravery" (Williams 1986:68).

Berdaches were "respected as a social group" among the Crow in the last century. They spent their time with women or each other, setting up their tipis in a separate area of the camp. "They called each other 'sister,' and saw Osh-Tisch as their leader" (Williams 1986:81).

Anthropologist Robert H. Lowie described Finds Them and Kills Them in 1912: "He is probably over fifty years of age, stands about 5 ft. 7 inches, and is of large build. According to several informants, former agents have repeatedly tried to make him don male clothes, but the other Indians themselves protested against

Finds Them and Kills Them (Crow).

Courtesy Museum of the American Indian, Heye Foundation, neg. no. 34256.

this, saying that it was against his nature. . . . He has the reputation of being very accomplished in feminine crafts" (1912:228).

When Williams asked Joe Medicine Crow about these attempts to force Finds Them and Kills Them to wear male clothes, Medicine Crow did not answer but had Williams meet him the next day, beneath the trees that surrounded the Bureau of Indian Affairs offices. While they strolled beneath the trees, Medicine Crow told Williams the following story:

> One agent in the late 1890s . . . tried to interfere with Osh-Tisch, who was the most respected *badé*. The agent incarcerated the *badés*, cut off their hair, made them wear men's clothing. He forced them to do manual labor, planting these trees that you see here on the BIA grounds. The people were so upset with this that Chief Pretty Eagle came into Crow Agency, and told [the agent] to leave the reservation. It was a tragedy, trying to change them. (1986:179)

Pressure to change came from Christian missionaries, as well. In 1903 a Baptist minister arrived on the reservation. According to Thomas Yellow Tail, he "condemned our traditions, including the *badé*. He told congregation members to stay away from Osh-Tisch and the other *badés*. He continued to condemn Osh-Tisch until his death. . . . That may be the reason why no others took up the *badé* role after Osh-Tisch died" (Williams 1986:183). According to Joe Medicine Crow, "Since then the younger ones dress like men and blend in more. There are some today, transvestites, homosexuals, or gays you call them, but they don't have any ceremonial role" (Williams 1986:224).

HASTIIN KLAH

NAVAJO

"Helping his people . . ."

Hastiin Klah (1867–1937) was one of the most famous Navajo medicine men and artists of all time. He was also a berdache, or *nadle*.

Hastiin Klah (Navajo).

Courtesy Wheelwright Museum of the American Indian, Santa Fe, New Mexico.

Klah began his training in Navajo ceremonial practice early in life. Because he was a *nadle,* he also learned to weave—normally women's work. He traveled extensively in the white world, demonstrating Navajo arts at world's fairs in Chicago in 1893 and 1933. Like the Zuni We'wha, Klah also met an American president—Franklin D. Roosevelt.

Klah formed close friendships with several white people interested in Navajo culture—in particular, Franc Newcomb, wife of a nearby trader, and Mary Cabot Wheelwright, a wealthy Bostonian. According to Wheelwright,

> I grew to respect and love him for his real goodness, generosity—and holiness, for there is no other word for it. He never had married, having spent twenty-five years studying not only the ceremonics he gave, but all the medicine lore of the tribe. . . . When I knew him he never kept anything for himself. It was hard to see him almost in rags at his ceremonies, but what was given him he seldom kept, passing it on to someone who needed it. . . . Our civilization and miracles he took simply without much wonder, as his mind was occupied with his religion and helping his people. . . . Everything was the outward form of the spirit world that was very real to him. (Wheelwright in Klah 1942:11–13)

Encouraged by Newcomb and Wheelwright, Klah was one of the first Navajos to weave religious sandpainting designs. His tapestries were eagerly purchased by art collectors in the 1920s and '30s, paving the way for today's recognition of Navajo weaving as a fine art.

Klah helped preserve Navajo religion, working with specialists to record his extensive knowledge. His culminating achievement was Mary Wheelwright's founding of the Wheelwright Museum in Santa Fe in 1937. Klah's ceremonial artifacts, weavings, and many recordings and transcriptions of the myths, songs, and ceremonies he knew became the core of the museum's collections.

SLAVE WOMAN
CHIPEWYAN

"She interpreted and persuaded until her voice was hoarse . . ."

The Indians of the far north of Canada formed a different relationship with Europeans than their southern counterparts. It wasn't their land that the Europeans wanted (until the past century), but the pelts of the region's fur-bearing animals. By learning to trap these animals for British and French traders, the Indians of the north formed a cooperative relationship with the newcomers. This allowed them to maintain their independent way of life, while enjoying new conveniences like guns, knives, and other goods.

Still, the impact of contact with foreigners led to widespread disruption of Canadian Indian life. Diseases, depletion of game, conflict between Indian groups in competition for land or trade, and conflict with Europeans decreased native populations and altered living patterns.

The first to gain guns, the Cree Indians became the dominant tribe of the far north, much as the Iroquois Confederacy had been to the south. They controlled access to trading posts and forced other tribes to trade with them as middlemen. They displaced the Chipewyans of the forests, and they pushed back the Sioux and Blackfeet onto the western plains.

In 1715 a group of Crees with a captive Chipewyan woman, came into York Factory, a British post on the western shore of Hudson Bay. The prisoner, known only as "Slave Woman," managed to speak with the post governor. She explained that if the Crees would stop their hostilities against the Chipewyans, her people would bring in many furs.

That June the governor sent Slave Woman, his assistant, William Stuart, and a band of 148 Crees to find the Chipewyans and escort them to the post to trade:

> The weather was very bad, and travel from east to west meant crossing many rivers and going around lakes or swamps. There was

> sickness, and the party divided into smaller groups. Stuart's party once went eight days without food, and found the bodies of some Chipewyans who had been shot by Crees while coming to trade. At this point the Crees with Stuart were afraid to go on, but Slave Woman persuaded them to wait for ten days while she went on alone. (Crowe 1974:78)

On the tenth day, just as the Crees were about to leave, Slave Woman returned. According to the description of this painting in the Hudson's Bay Company Archives, Slave Woman arrived "with a large body of her countrymen prepared for war. Four hundred of them remained in the rear, while a party of 160 remained within hailing distance of the Cree camp. . . . The woman advanced with only two of her compatriots."

Slave Woman "interpreted and persuaded until her voice was hoarse" (Crowe 1974:78). Finally, after two days, the Crees and Chipewyans had a feast of friendship. This laid the foundation for peace. As the governor at York wrote, "The Slave Woman was the chief instrument in finishing of it."

In 1717 the British founded a post on the Churchill River to expand their Chipewyan trade. Slave Woman wanted to continue visiting other tribes to extend the peace she had established, even if it meant leaving her family, but she fell ill at the new post and died there. Nonetheless, as a result of the peace she negotiated, the fur trade moved quickly into new areas of the north and west (Crowe 1974:78).

Women became hunters, warriors, mediators, and even chiefs in many tribes of North America. Some were female berdaches—they lived and dressed like men and married other women. But in many cases, information about these women's personal and sexual lives is not available. While not all women warriors and chiefs can be considered female berdaches, their heroism, service, and devotion to their communities provide role models for all contemporary American Indian women, lesbian and heterosexual alike.

Slave Woman (Chipewyan).

Painting by Franklin Arbuckle (1953),

Courtesy Hudson's Bay Company Head Office Photograph Collection, Hudson's Bay Company Archives, Provincial Archives of Manitoba.

PINE LEAF

CROW

"She seemed incapable of fear . . ."

The son of a white Southerner and a black woman, Jim Beckwourth was born a slave. When his father emancipated him in the 1820s, Beckwourth traveled to the Rocky Mountains and spent the rest of his life there as a trapper, trader, scout, and adventurer. In 1828 he joined the Crow Indians, distinguished himself as a warrior, and for a time, served as a war chief. It was during this period that he met a Crow woman called Pine Leaf.

According to Beckwourth, Pine Leaf ("in Indian, Bar-chee-am-pe") was "one of the bravest women that ever lived. . . . She possessed great intellectual powers. She was endowed with extraordinary muscular strength, with the activity of the cat and the speed of the antelope" (Beckwourth 1931:133).

When her twin brother was killed during a raid on their village, Pine Leaf "solemnly vowed that she would never marry until she had killed a hundred of the enemy with her own hand. . . . Whenever a war-party started, Pine Leaf was the first to volunteer to accompany them. . . . She seemed incapable of fear; and when she arrived at womanhood, could fire a gun without flinching, and use the Indian weapons with as great dexterity as the most accomplished warrior" (Beckwourth 1931:133).

After serving with her on several war parties, Beckwourth asked Pine Leaf to marry him. She responded, "Do you suppose I would break my vow to the Great Spirit? He sees and knows all things; he would be angry with me, and would not suffer me to live to avenge my brother's death."

When Beckwourth persisted, she replied, "Well, I will marry you."

"When we return?"

"No; but when the pine-leaves turn yellow" (Beckwourth 1931:134).

Pine Leaf (Crow).

From T. D. Bonner, ed., The Life and Adventures of James P. Beckwourth . . . *(New York: Harper and Bros., 1856).*

Several days passed before Beckwourth realized that pine leaves do not turn yellow.

Some experts have challenged the accuracy of Beckwourth's acount of Pine Leaf. But Robert Lowie noted that "every once in a while the genuineness of the record is forcibly demonstrated, as when a maiden promised to marry Beckwourth 'when the pine leaves turn yellow,' an expression still in vogue" (Lowie 1935: 335).

Even if Pine Leaf's story was fictionalized, it is remarkably similar to that of Woman Chief, a Crow warrior woman whose life *is* well documented. Two frontiersmen, Edwin Denig and Rudolph

Kurz, knew Woman Chief personally (see Denig 1953, 1961; Kurz 1937; Medicine 1983). Denig wrote, "As in the case of the Berdêche [berdache] who, being male inclined to female pursuits, so this child, reversing the position, desired to acquire manly accomplishments." She was "taller and stronger than most women," and "long before she had ventured on the warpath she could rival any of the young men in all their amusements and occupations, was a capital shot with the rifle, and would spend most of her time in killing deer and bighorn, which she butchered and carried home on her back when hunting on foot" (Denig 1961:196).

Woman Chief became a warrior when a party of Blackfeet attacked her village. Taking up her gun, she killed several of the enemy while escaping injury herself. Within a year she was leading her own war parties. "In every battle . . . some gallant act distinguished her. . . . The Indians seemed to be proud of her [and] sung forth her praise in songs composed by them after each of her brave deeds" (Denig 1961:198).

After a time Woman Chief married another woman. Denig commented, "Strange country this, where males assume the dress and perform the duties of females, while women turn men and mate with their own sex!" (Denig 1961:199) Eventually Woman Chief supported *four* wives.

For twenty years Woman Chief "conducted herself well in all things appertaining to war and a hunter's life" (Denig 1961:199). But in 1854, when she undertook to visit the Crow's long-time enemies, the Gros Ventres, she was killed in a surprise attack.

RUNNING EAGLE

BLACKFEET

"I shall never marry . . ."

In the late nineteenth century, James Willard Schultz befriended the Blackfeet Indians of Montana. The Blackfeet adopted him into the tribe and gave him the name Apikun'i. Schultz wrote several popular books about the Blackfeet and promoted Indian lore through groups like the Boy Scouts. In 1919 he published *Run-*

Running Eagle (Blackfeet).
From James Willard Schultz, Running Eagle: The Warrior Girl *(Boston: Houghton Mifflin, 1919).*

ning Eagle: The Warrior Girl, the story of the "virgin woman warrior" of the Blackfeet.

Schultz was told the story of Running Eagle by Tail-Feathers-Coming-Over-the-Hill, who had grown up with her in the first half of the nineteenth century. Even as a girl, Running Eagle rejected female activities and begged her father to make her a bow and arrows. She was nicknamed *sakwo'mapi akikwan,* or "boy-girl" (Schultz 1919:38). When her mother insisted that she take up lodge work, Running Eagle replied: "I wish that I was a boy . . . but if I cannot be one, I can at least do a boy's work. I shall not tan hides, I shall not do lodge work, I shall continue to help my father!" (Schultz 1919:11). Running Eagle's father allowed her to join him on hunting expeditions, and soon she gained a reputation for both skill and courage.

When her father was killed by the Crows and her mother died soon after, Running Eagle insisted on maintaining her own lodge, taking on the role of both father and mother for her younger brothers and sisters: "I care not what people say of me so long as I do right. As for marrying . . . I shall never marry! I shall never be any man's slave!" (Schultz 1919:79).

Running Eagle took in a "tall, slender, fine-looking woman" named Suya'ki to look after the children and help with the lodge work. Suya'ki had been mistreated by a recently deceased husband and "wanted nothing more to do with men" (Schultz 1919:86). This freed Running Eagle for hunting. "Buffaloes, elk, deer, antelopes, all fell before her sure aim, and her lodge was always rich with meat, well-tanned buffalo robes, leather and furs for trade" (Schultz 1919:92).

When a war party was formed to take revenge on the Crow Indians for the death of her father, Running Eagle insisted on joining it. On their return, she single-handedly saved a herd of horses from capture by the Crows. Her companions immediately proclaimed her "Girl Chief" and "Medicine Girl" (Schultz 1919:142). She was twenty years old (Schultz 1916:13).

Running Eagle began to dress in men's clothing while on war parties. Like a man, she gave feasts and dances—"the greatest chiefs and warriors came to them, and were glad to be there" (Schultz 1916:17). At the same time, her lodge became "a visiting-place for many girls, young married women, and not a few old women. . . . They all came to her with their troubles" (Schultz 1919:156). "The general opinion of the camp . . . was now this: the gods had implanted in her a nature far different from that of any other girl that had ever lived. She was neither to be judged nor governed by the tribal laws regarding women. She was to be honored and respected for what she had done" (Schultz 1919:177).

Running Eagle had the other women "tell it around for me that I shall never marry, that my life is for a purpose other than being the head of some man's lodge. Say that I want to be a friend to all, that I want all to look upon me as a sister and nothing else"

(Schultz 1919:178). Even so, Blackfeet, Crow, and Assiniboine men longed for her hand. "Never, never had they seen a woman so beautiful, so graceful as she was in her gorgeous man's war costume" (Schultz 1919:294).

Running Eagle went on nine raids and counted coup three times before she was killed herself, sometime in the 1840s (Schultz 1916:20). A hundred years later Ewers found Blackfeet elders who still recalled stories of her exploits (Ewers in Denig 1961:200).

WOMEN HUNTERS

"Dexterity and courage . . ."

In 1837 Alfred Jacob Miller joined an expedition to the west and became one of the first American artists to depict the Rocky Mountains. The pictures he painted of the Indians and Indian life of that region are a valuable record.

Two of Miller's paintings depict Indian women performing what were usually male activities: hunting buffalo and catching horses. Although he does not identify her tribe, Miller provides a description of a female buffalo hunter:

> To win renown amongst the Indians and adventurers of the Far West, the first step is that of being a successful hunter. Every one at all ambitious strives to this end, and as the fever is catching;—An Indian woman at intervals starts up who is capable of running and bringing down a Buffalo. . . .
>
> No sooner does she reach the animal than she must watch his every movement,—keep an eye to her horse and guide him,—must look out for rifts and Buffalo wallows on the prairies,—guard against the animal's forming an angle and goring,—manage bow and arrows, or lance—and while both are at full speed to wound him in a vital part;—To do all this requires great presence of mind, dexterity, and courage,—and few women are found amongst them willing to undertake or capable of performing it. (Miller 1951:90)

Women Hunters.

Painting by Alfred Jacob Miller (c. 1837).

Courtesy Walters Art Gallery, Baltimore.

KUILIY
PEND D'OREILLE

"Renown for intrepidity . . ."

The Pend d'Oreille (or Kalispel) and Flathead (or Salish) tribes are related by language, culture, and history. Traditional allies, today they share a reservation in western Montana.

With the introducton of the horse, these tribes began to venture across the continental divide to hunt buffalo on the plains. Here they competed with the larger, more powerful Blackfeet tribes. In the late 1700s the Blackfeet acquired guns and threatened to cut off all access to the plains.

Outnumbered, with only bows and arrows, the tribes of western Montana adopted a threefold strategy—military, diplomatic, and religious. The Flatheads established direct trade with Americans and British to obtain arms, and they pursued alliances with whites—in contrast to the Blackfeet, who were resolutely hostile to intruders. Finally, to compensate for their smaller numbers, they sought supernatural aid (Ewers 1948:14–19).

The Flatheads had learned of an especially promising source of assistance: the "Blackrobes," or Catholic priests. In the 1830s they sent a series of expeditions to St. Louis, Missouri, to request missionaries. Finally, in 1841, Fathers Pierre Jean De Smet, Nicholas Point, and Gregory Mengarini made the long trek to western Montana.

At first, some decisive victories against the Blackfeet convinced the Flatheads and Pend d'Oreilles that the spiritual power of the Blackrobes was good war medicine. But when the missionaries began to insist on radical changes in the economic, social, and sexual life of the tribes, attitudes began to change (Ewers 1948:19–22).

One father complained that the Flatheads and Pend d'Oreilles continued to give "themselves up to their old war-dances, to savage obscenity and to shameless excesses of the flesh" (Ravalli in Garraghan 1938:377). When the missionaries scolded them with "fatherly rebukes" and "exhortations," the Indians pitched their

Kuiliy (Pend d'Oreille).
From Nicolas Point, Wilderness Kingdom: Indian Life in the Rocky Mountains, 1840–1847, *trans. Joseph P. Donnelly (New York: Holt, Rinehart and Winston, 1967).*

tents away from the mission "with a view to do what the Fathers forbade them to do"—that is, gambling and dancing "with all its besetting indecencies" (Ravalli and Accolti in Garraghan 1938: 377, 383, 380). As relations worsened, the Flatheads refused to sell the priests provisions. In 1850 the mission was abandoned and remained so for the next sixteen years.

Father Point seems to have been more tolerant toward native lifeways. He traveled with the tribes on two of their hunts, and he painted a candid series of pictures documenting their life. He even described and illustrated Flathead and Pend d'Oreille women taking part in warfare. Point relates an occasion in 1842 when a small group of Pend d'Oreilles cornered a larger group of

Blackfeet. According to his informant, "Fortunately for us the shots had been heard by the camp and all the Pend d'Oreilles warriors rode out, led by Kuiliy, a young Pend d'Oreille woman renowned for intrepidity on the field of battle. They pounced on the Blackfeet we had cornered" (Point 1967:158).

Point's caption for this illustration reads, "A woman warrior's swift about-face left the enemy stupefied" (156).

EVER SINCE THE WORLD BEGAN: BERDACHE MYTHS AND TALES

A DESIRE IN THE CHILD'S HEART

MOHAVE

Through oral literature—myths, folktales, stories, poetry, and music—North American Indians expressed not only their world view but their ideas about how things got to be the way they are. Traditional oral literature served many of the same purposes as the disciplines of theology, psychology, sociology, and natural science in western culture.

One body of oral literature—called origin myths—is especially concerned with beginnings and sources of things. Origin myths answer such questions as: How was the world made and why? How did our tribe come to live in this place, with these customs? Why do humans, animals, plants, and the forces of nature behave as they do?

Because male and female berdaches were a part of so many tribes, it's not surprising that origin myths answer questions about them, as well. Why do some individuals become berdaches? What is their place in the social and supernatural order?

Here is how the Mohave—a Southwest tribe who live along the Colorado River in Arizona and California—accounted for their berdaches. The transcriber, George Devereux, translates the Mohave word for berdache as "transvestite."

Ever since the world began at the magic mountain Avi-kwame· it was said that there would be transvestites. In the beginning, if

Reprinted from George Devereux, "Institutionalized Homosexuality of the Mohave Indians,"* Human Biology *9 (1937):503–504.

they were to become transvestites, the process started during their intra-uterine life. When they grew up they were given toys according to their sex. They did not like these toys however. At the beginning, the God Matavilye died at Avi-kwame·, not because he had to die, but because he wanted to set mankind an example. There is the house. He is on his death-bed and people are all around him. He tells them that their lives would be different, and some among them would turn into transvestites. Then Matavilye died. All the people went their own way but Matavilye loved mankind so much that, although he was already on his way to heaven, he returned to be cremated in our fashion. Had he not returned to us, we would have been just like the Whites: evil, cruel and grasping. He cared for us so much that he returned to be cremated on earth. If a ghost comes to visit the earth he does it because he likes the earth very much. If from underneath the cremation pit a whirlwind rises, it means a soul went in there, because it thought so much of the earth. Then all things begin in that death-house. When there is a desire in a child's heart to become a transvestite that child will act different. It will let people become aware of that desire. They may insist on giving the child the toys and garments of its true sex, but the child will throw them away and do this every time there is a big gathering. Then people prepare a skirt of shredded bark for the boy or a breech-clout for the girl. If they give them the garments worn by other members of their sex they will turn away from them. They do all they can to dissuade girls who show such inclinations. But if they fail to convince her they will realize that it cannot be helped. She will be chumming with men and be one of them. Then all those who have tried to change her conduct will gather and agree that they had done all that could be done and that the only thing for them to do was to give her the status of a transvestite. These female transvestites *(hwame·)* are like lewd women who also throw away their housekeeping implements, and run wild.

RITES OF PASSAGE

MOHAVE

Among the Mohave, a formal initiation rite marked the transition into berdache status. The anthropologist Alfred Kroeber recorded the following account of these rites, which includes some of the songs used in the proceedings.

The Mohave call transvestites *alyha* and hold a ceremony inducting youths into this condition. They say that a boy dreams that he is an *alyha* and then can not do otherwise. Four men who have dreamed about the ceremony are sent for, and spend the night in the house, twisting cords and gathering shredded bark for the skirt the prospective *alyha* will thereafter wear. The youth himself lies, with two women sitting by him. As they twist the cords, the men sing:

ihatnya vudhi -------------------- roll it this way.
ihatnya va'ama ------------------ roll it that way.

When the petticoat nears completion:

istum ----------------------------- I hold it.
icham ----------------------------- I place it.
hilyuvik ------------------------- it is done.
havirk ---------------------------- it is finished.
ka'avek -------------------------- hear!
kidhauk -------------------------- listen!

These songs the singers dreamed when they were with the god Mastamho, and during the night they tell and sing of how they saw him ordering the first performance of this ceremony.

In the morning the two women lift the youth and take him outdoors. One of the singers puts on the skirt and dances to the river in four stops, the youth following and imitating. Then all bathe. Thereupon the two women give the youth the front and back pieces of his new dress and paint his face white. After four days he

Reprinted from Alfred L. Kroeber, "Handbook of the Indians of California," Bureau of American Ethnology Bulletin *78 (1925): 748–49.*

is painted again and then is an *alyha*. Such persons speak, laugh, smile, sit, and act like women. They are lucky at gambling, say the Mohave, but die young. It is significant that a variety of venereal sickness which they treat is also called *alyha*.

BERDACHE CULTURE BEARER

TIPAI

The origin myth of the Tipai or Kamia, who lived in the Imperial Valley of southern California, includes a supernatural berdache (or "hermaphrodite") who appears with two companions. According to Edward Gifford, who recorded the myth, "These were the introducers of Kamia culture" (1931: 12). They came from the sacred mountain Wikami—*which is also revered by the Mohave, Yuma, and the Ipai, or Diegueño Indians. (The Mohave name is* Avikwami.)

Later there came from the mountain Wikami three persons who were to be the Kamia leaders. They were a hermaphrodite [described by the informant as half man, half woman] called Warharmi [cf. Mohave *hwami*] and her twin "sons" [not really her sons, Narpai said], both called Madkwahomai. These three had learned much at Wikami. They came south along the Colorado River. They found the feathers of birds which had died, as they traveled along day after day. The feathers were of the birds kak (crow), tokwil, and kusaul. The three travelers made headdresses of these feathers and painted their faces as for war. They brought bows, arrows, and clubs.

From the Colorado River at Yuma they crossed over to Imperial Valley. Their appearance so frightened the Kamia that they fled in all directions. One Kamia woman did not flee before the three. She was married by one of the Madkwahomai twins. Then the three newcomers and the woman settled at Saxnuwai.

Reprinted from Edward Winslow Gifford, "The Kamia of Imperial Valley," Bureau of American Ethnology Bulletin *97 (1931): 79–80.*

The seeds of maize and beans had been given them by Mastamho. These the three travelers brought from Wikami and planted at Saxnuwai, thus introducing cultivation in the Imperial Valley. Those Diegueño who had gone to the mountains to live failed to receive the seeds. The three travelers brought the seeds of certain wild plants as well.

At Saxnuwai, Warharmi and the twins planted, for they found wet ground there. Before their departure from Wikami Mastamho had explained how everything was to be done. He had said that Warharmi and the two Madkwahomai were to be farmers and that they should go to dwell among the Kamia, whom Mastamho had sent to live on the shores of the Salton Sea.

HOW THE SALMON WERE BROUGHT TO THIS WORLD

BELLA COOLA

The Bella Coola Indians of British Columbia lived in the narrow valley of the Bella Coola River. They fished the river and the sea and supplemented their diet with foods gathered from the forests and mountainsides.

Berries, in great abundance and variety, appeared in the summer and were a source of pleasure and an occasion for thanksgiving. According to anthropologist T. F. McIlwraith, "All women can pick berries, but in every village there is at least one who has the prerogative of picking the first of every kind" (1948a:265). Sometimes a berdache was assigned the status of First Berry Picker. In fact, in the following myth, which describes the origin of foods, a supernatural berdache is responsible for bringing berries to the land of the Bella Coola.

This figure is called Skheents, *and, according to McIlwraith, "His face is that of a woman, his voice that of a woman, but he has masculine characteristics as well" (1948b:179). He is portrayed in a masked dance as the protector of twelve*

Reprinted from Franz Boas, "The Mythology of the Bella Coola Indians," Memoirs of the American Museum of Natural History *2(2) (1898):38–40.*

supernatural maidens. This myth, recorded by Franz Boas in the 1890s, describes the actions of this supernatural berdache, or, in Boas's translation, "hermaphrodite."

Once upon a time a man named Winwī'na lived at Q'ō'mqūtis. One day he was sitting in front of his house, looking at the river. He thought, "I wish fish would ascend this river." At that time not a single salmon visited Bella Coola River. Winwī'na entered his house and lay down, thinking about the salmon. One night while he was asleep he dreamt that with the help of all the animals he had made war upon the salmon, that he had vanquished them, and that since that time the salmon had ascended Bella Coola River. When he awoke he invited all the animals to his house, and told them about his dream. They all came, and when they had entered he shut the door. Then he spoke: "My brothers, I have invited you to my house that you may hear what I wish to do. You shall help me to obtain what I desire." The Mink asked him in what they were to assist him; and he replied, "I want to go to Mīa'ltoa. There is not a single fish in our river, and I dreamt that with your help I vanquished the fish. Let us make war upon them. I shall certainly take some slaves, and we will place them in this river." Mink retorted, "I am glad that you are speaking in regard to this matter. I asked my father the Sun to give us salmon, and I think he gave you the dream which you told us."

All the birds agreed, and they resolved to start as soon as possible. Then Winwī'na asked Masmasalā'nix to build a canoe. The latter complied with his request, and made a self-moving canoe, to which he gave the names "WinaiōtstūLs" and "Kunkunu-'qtstuLs." In the third moon after the winter solstice the canoe was completed, and Winwī'na started, accompanied by the clouds, the birds, and by all the animals. The Hermaphrodite was sitting in the stern of the canoe. They went down the fiord; and when they passed the village of Bella Bella, they saw the Cormorant sitting on the beach, who asked to be taken along as a passenger. They travelled westward for a long time, and finally they reached the country of the Salmon. They saw that there were no trees. The country was a vast prairie. A large sun was shining in the sky.

Soon they descried the village of the Salmon. They sent out the Raven as a spy. When he returned, he told them that in the evening the Salmon were in the habit of playing on the beach. Mink suggested that this would be the best time for carrying some of them away. Then the Crane (according to another version, the Hawk) said, "I shall carry away the Sockeye Salmon." The Wren said, "I shall carry away the Humpback Salmon." The Kingfisher (according to another version, the Crane) said, "I shall carry away the Dog Salmon." The Raven said, "I shall carry away the Silver Salmon." The Fish-Hawk said, "I shall carry away the Olachen and the Salmon Trout." The Cloud said, "I shall carry away the Spring Salmon." Finally the Cormorant said, "I am only a passenger, and I will take whatever I can get." The Mink remarked, "I will not say what I am going to carry away: I only want to tell you that you must each take one male and one female. Now start. You are invisible to the Salmon. When you approach them, they will not be able to see you, just as we cannot see the ghosts, even when they are walking by our side." They left Winwī'na to guard the canoe. Then all the birds and the Mink took each one male and one female child of various kinds of fish. When they carried them off, the children fainted, as though their souls had been taken away. Their bodies remained at the place where they had been playing. The Salmon did not see their captors, and did not know why the children were fainting. The birds returned to the canoe, carrying the fish. Then Winwī'na said, "Let us go on and see what is beyond the country of the Salmon." Soon they arrived at a place called Qoalē'nia (this name is not quite certain), in which vast numbers of berries were growing. Here the Hermaphrodite went ashore, and picked all kinds of berries, which she carried into the canoe. Then they returned home. For seven months they had staid in the country of the Salmon. They reached the coast shortly after the winter solstice (?). When they passed Bella Bella, the Cormorant said, "This is my home. I will go ashore here." He went, and took along the Salmon which he had captured. Ever since that time there are salmon at Bella Bella. The others travelled on, and came to the mouth of Bella Coola River. Then they threw all the various kinds of fish into the water. The Salmon jumped, and began to ascend the river. Then

Winwī'na arose in his canoe and told each at what season he was to arrive. He scattered the berries over the mountains and through the valleys, and told them at what season to ripen. After he had done so, he invited his companions into his house, and gave them a feast.

A CONFLICT OF THE SEXES

NAVAJO

A key episode of the Navajo origin myth centers around a dispute between men and women. The causes of this discord vary in the different versions of the myth, but the sequence of events is similar. Conflict leads the men and women to separate. When one side fares better than the other, a reunion is proposed. The men and women rejoin, but with a new understanding of their responsibilities toward each other.

The Navajo berdache, or nadle, *has two key roles in these accounts. First, before separating from the women, the men seek* nadle *advice. Second, because a* nadle *joins the men, they get along better on their own than the women and outlast them.*

In the following account recorded by Aileen O'Bryan, sex is the source of discord.

After First Man found his wife with another he would not come out to speak to the people. The black cloud rose higher, but First Man would not leave his dwelling; neither would he eat or drink. No one spoke to the people for four days. All during this time First Man remained silent, and would not touch food or water. Four times the white cloud rose. Then the four chiefs went to First Man and demanded to know why he would not speak to the people. The chiefs asked this question three times, and a fourth, before First Man would answer them.

He told them to bring him an emetic. This he took and purified

Reprinted from Aileen O'Bryan, "The Dîné: Origin Myths of the Navaho Indians," Bureau of American Ethnology Bulletin *163 (1956):7–8.*

himself. First Man then asked them to send the hermaphrodite [*nadle*] to him. When he came First Man asked him if the metate and brush were his. He said that they were. First Man asked him if he could cook and prepare food like a woman, if he could weave, and brush the hair. And when he had assured First Man that he could do all manner of woman's work, First Man said: "Go and prepare food and bring it to me." After he had eaten, First Man told the four chiefs what he had seen, and what his wife had said.

At this time the Great-Coyote-Who-Was-Formed-in-the-Water came to First Man and told him to cross the river. They made a big raft and crossed at the place where the Male River followed through the Female River. And all the male beings left the female beings on the river bank; and as they rowed across the river they looked back and saw that First Woman and the female beings were laughing. They were also behaving very wickedly.

In the beginning the women did not mind being alone. They cleared and planted a small field. On the other side of the river First Man and the chiefs hunted and planted their seeds. They had a good harvest. Nadle ground the corn and cooked the food. Four seasons passed. The men continued to have plenty and were happy; but the women became lazy, and only weeds grew on their land. The women wanted fresh meat. Some of them tried to join the men and were drowned in the river.

First Woman made a plan. As the women had no way to satisfy their passions, some fashioned long narrow rocks, some used the feathers of the turkey, and some used strange plants (cactus). First Woman told them to use these things. One woman brought forth a big stone. This stone-child was later the Great Stone that rolled over the earth killing men. Another woman brought forth the Big Birds of Tsa bida'hi; and others gave birth to the giants and monsters who later destroyed many people.

On the opposite side of the river the same condition existed. The men, wishing to satisfy their passions, killed the females of mountain sheep, lion, and antelope. Lightning struck these men. When First Man learned of this he warned his men that they would all be killed. He told them that they were indulging in a dangerous practice. Then the second chief spoke: he said that life was hard and that it was a pity to see women drowned. He asked why they should not bring the women across the river and all live together again.

"Now we can see for ourselves what comes from our wrong doing," he said. "We will know how to act in the future." The three other chiefs of the animals agreed with him, so First Man told them to go and bring the women.

After the women had been brought over the river First Man spoke: "We must be purified," he said. "Everyone must bathe. The men must dry themselves with white cornmeal, and the women, with yellow."

This they did, living apart for four days. After the fourth day First Woman came and threw her right arm around her husband. She spoke to the others and said that she could see her mistakes, but with her husband's help she would henceforth lead a good life. Then all the male and female beings came and lived with each other again.

THE BATTLE OF THE STO-RO-KA AND THE KA-TSI-NA

ACOMA-LAGUNA

The Pueblo Indians of New Mexico are known as villagers and farmers, but in traditional times hunting was an equally important source of food. The Pueblos viewed farming and hunting as opposites, however. Agriculture was a life-nurturing process and successful farming required care, patience, and gentleness. Hunting involved the taking of life, and it required strength, aggression, and violence.

In the following myth from Acoma and Laguna, this conflict is symbolized by two groups of supernatural beings who fight a war. One side uses bows made with strings of plant fibers—symbolizing agriculture. The other side has bow strings of antelope sinews—symbolizing hunting. At the end of the story, these two principles are unified and brought into balance.

Reprinted from John M. Gunn, Schat-Chen: History, Traditions and Narratives of the Queres Indians of Laguna and Acoma *(Albuquerque: Albright and Anderson, 1916), p. 173.*

The balance of gender—male and female—is another theme in the story. One of the warring sides, the Storoka, is described as a race of kokwima*—the Acoma-Laguna word for berdache. These supernatural berdaches wear women's dresses with men's pants beneath. Combining male and female traits, the Storoka symbolize the original unity of the sexes.*

The Sto-ro-ka or Kur-ret-ti-ku, are described as a race of Ko-quima, or Hermaphrodites. They occupied the country in the vicinity of the lake that is known to the Qe-res as the Arrosauk, situated south of Flagstaff, Arizona.

The Ka-tsi-na warred against the Sto-ro-ka and were defeated in a severe battle fought north of the Zuni Salt Lake.

The Sto-ro-ka went into the battle with bow strings made from the fibers of the soap weed, while those of the Ka-tsi-na were of deer and antelope sinews. While the battle was in progress, a terrific storm of rain and hail came down upon the warriors. The bow strings of the Ka-tsi-na were wet by the rain and soon became limp and useless; while those of the Sto-ro-ka, being made of vegetable fiber, were only rendered more tense and consequently more efficient by the wetting.

Thus, by the aid of the storm, the Sto-ro-ka were victorious in the battle, and soon brought the Ka-tsi-na to sue for peace. A treaty was agreed upon between the chiefs. In order to preserve this treaty, the headman of the Ka-tsi-na had a history of the fight and the conditions of the treaty inscribed upon the side of a smooth sandstone bluff. Below the writing were drawn, in outline, three deer, two bucks and a doe. This was the emblem of the Ka-tsi-na.

DOUBLE WOMAN

LAKOTA

Among the Lakota and other plains tribes, individuals looked to dreams and visions for personal and spiritual inspiration. A

Reprinted by permission of the University of Nebraska Press from James R. Walker, Lakota Belief and Ritual, *ed. Raymond J. DeMallie and Elaine A. Jahner (Lincoln: University of Nebraska Press, 1980), pp. 165–66.*

powerful vision provided supernatural aid and directed the individual toward a particular lifestyle. A warrior, for example, sought dreams that would make him courageous and invincible in battle.

But if a young man had the "wrong vision"—that is, if he dreamed of women's symbols or female supernaturals—his way in life would be that of the berdache. Double Woman was the supernatural who most often appeared to berdaches. She conferred skills in arts, crafts, medicine, and healing.

But what if a woman *had this dream? What did such a vision confer to her?*

The following account from the Lakota Thomas Tyon describes the influence of Double Woman in such cases. In fact, the women who dreamed of Double Woman shared many traits with male berdaches—except, instead of specializing in domestic work like male berdaches, they took up the work of men. As Paula Gunn Allen has pointed out, this account describes a remarkable bonding rite in which two women "become united by the power of wiya numpa," *or Double Woman (Allen 1981:82).*

When a woman dreams of the Double Woman, from that time on, in everything she makes, no one excels her. But then the woman is very much like a crazy woman *(lila witkowin)*. She laughs uncontrollably and so time and time again she acts deceptively *(knayan xkinyelo)*. So the people are very afraid of her. She causes all men who stand near her to become possessed *(wicayuknaxkin)*. For that reason these women are called Double Women. They are very promiscuous *(lila hinknatunpi s'a,* repeatedly have many husbands). But then in the things they make nobody excels them. They do much quillwork. From then on, they are very skillful. They also do work like a man.

The Double Woman is frequently at rocky cliffs. First, people hear their voices, it is said. After that, the first thing that happens is that they dream of the Double Woman, they say. Whoever dreams, she herself, sometimes imitates her in the camp circle *(hocokagapelo)*. When the camp is in a circle, she goes around the inside of the circle. Two women [Double Woman dreamers] go all the way around the circle from their home bound together by a single rope. And in the middle of the rope, they tie up an imitation of a baby. And bearing it, they go along laughing uncontrollably. Therefore, they cause all the men who stand near them to become possessed *(iyuhawica yuknaxkinyanpi)*. This is the song they sing as they walk along. "Someone is meeting me here," they say. And then, "He is the one!" they say. And then they laugh uncontrollably. So they cause all the young men to become possessed, it is said. I myself, personally, have never seen it. I have heard them tell about it. Even now, they believe these things are *wakan* [holy].

Then too, some Double Women are doctors. Whoever walks about at night is very afraid of these Double Woman dreamers. They do not wish to hear their voices. They are very afraid of the night. Nobody sees them but they do not want to hear their voices. When they hear the voices, only women dream about the Double Woman; men never dream of her. Whoever dreams in this way seems to be crazy *(witkotkoke selececa)* but then everything she makes is very beautiful. Well, so it is. They believe them to be *wakan*. This is the end.

COYOTE, FOX, AND PANTHER

OKANAGON

The remaining selections fall into the category of Trickster tales. Coyote is the most famous Trickster in North America, and most tribes have their own versions of Coyote's pranks and exploits. But there are other Tricksters in American Indian literature, as well, as the next three stories show.

Sexual jokes and humorous episodes of mistaken identity occur when Trickster changes or combines genders. The following stories highlight such common human failings as lust, vanity, and greed, and they show how individuals get their come-uppance when these desires get the better of them. The sexual Trickster also reveals American Indian attitudes toward gender and

Reprinted from James A. Teit, "Okanagon Tales," Memoirs of the American Folk-Lore Society *11 (1917):75–76.*

identity. These are not fixed traits. As one went through life it was possible to have many different identities and sometimes, like the Trickster and the berdache, even change one's gender.

Coyote and Fox were living together. They were friends, and always had plenty to eat. Fox used to procure game, for he was a good hunter. Once upon a time he had bad luck, and could not get any game. Perhaps he had been bewitched. The friends began to starve. Fox said to Coyote, "You are powerful and gifted. Try to break our spell of bad luck, so that we may procure game." Coyote did not answer. For three days, when he came back from hunting, Fox repeated his request. Fox thought, "Coyote will do something foolish." The fourth night Fox spoke again. Early the following morning Coyote arose, and went to wash himself at a spring near by. He returned to the lodge, went to his pillow, and drew from under it his comb and paint-pouch. He did not speak, but dressed his hair and painted his face after the manner of women. Then he dressed himself and left the house without saying a word. He travelled about aimlessly. At last he came to the houses of many people, whose chief was Panther. Coyote asked for Panther's house, and the people pointed it out to him. He went in, and sat down alongside of Panther. He said, "I do not come here for nothing, chief. My father and mother sent me here to marry you." Panther answered, "I do not desire to act contrary to the pleasure of your parents. I will not decline their offer, if they have chosen me as their son-in-law."

Night came, and Panther asked Coyote to go to bed with him. When they were in bed, Coyote drew away from him, saying, "I am a maiden and have never known man. I am afraid and ashamed. I am also thinking of my parents. If you will give me a pack of food to take to my parents three successive days, I will be yours. By that time my parents will be supplied with food, so that I shall not have to worry about them, and I shall have become used to you." Panther agreed to this, and on the following morning Coyote carried a pack of food to his starving younger brother.

Prairie-Chicken, who was a wise person, was living among these people. He said to the others, "Our chief is a great man, but he has made a grave mistake. His wife is not a woman, she is Coyote." This was the third day, and Coyote had returned from carrying his third load to his home. He knew what Prairie-Chicken had said. Now, Prairie-Chicken and others made a sweat-house, and invited Panther to sweat with them. They were going to tell him who his wife really was, and they intended to purify him. When Panther was inside, and they were about to tell him who his wife was, Coyote ran about above the sweat-house and howled like a coyote. He shouted, "You will never have a good wife, Panther, you bad warrior, you bad man of the warpath!" Panther was ashamed, and said nothing.

DOUBLE-SEX

NAVAJO

The Navajo god Bego chidii *was a* nadle, *or berdache. As this tale reveals, in Navajo philosophy being double-sexed meant being doubly sexual.*

Be′gočidí was the son of the sun. The sun committed adultery with everything in the world. That was how so many monsters were born. After this, the sun was put a way off so that this could not happen again. But as the sun came up he touched a flower which became pregnant and gave birth to Be′gočidí. He was the youngest son of the sun, and the sun spoiled him. He was put in control of many things, such as game and domestic animals. He was a berdache and the first pottery-maker.

He could also move about invisibly and change into different forms at will: a rainbow, wind, sand, water, etc. He was named Be′gočidí because he would make himself invisible and sneak up on young girls to touch their breasts, shouting "be′go be′go" (breast). He especially annoyed men who were hunting. When a hunter had taken his aim and was ready to shoot, Be′gočidí would

Reprinted from Willard W. Hill, "The Agricultural and Hunting Methods of the Navaho Indians," Yale University Publications in Anthropology *18 (1938): 8.*

sneak up behind him, grab his testicles, and shout "be'go." This spoiled the hunter's aim every time. The worst was when a man and woman lay down to have intercourse. He was always touching one or the other and shouting "be'go."

THE HEHE'YA TRICK HÜI'KI

HOPI

The Hehe'ya kachina is known to most of the Pueblo tribes of the Southwest as a humorous and clumsy bumbler. In the Hopi villages, the Hehe'ya kachinas wear a sheepskin in the style of a woman's dress. They carry lariats and sometimes lasso unwitting spectators, threatening to take them away—all with a great deal of hilarity.

This tale describes the Hehe'ya as* siwahova. *A footnote by the transcriber, Alexander Stephan, defines this as "a man that no woman will marry" (1929:34).* Hova *is the Hopi word for berdache.

At Kishyu'ba dwelt the Hü'iki kachina. The Hehe'ya are industrious, but they are *siwahova.* The Hüi'ki were one day working in their fields and the Hehe'ya came to help them. About noon, the Hü'iki being hungry said to the Hehe'ya, "Go you to the village and tell our wives to give you some food and bring some out to us," and as they were starting on this errand the Hüi'ki said, "By what name are you people known, how shall we call you?" The Hehe'ya said, "We are called *i'ich chova* (hasten to copulate)." When they reached the village they found the women preparing wafer-bread and other food, and having delivered their message, the women set food before them, and made bundles of food for them to take out to the fields. After the Hehe'ya had eaten, they said to the women, "Your husbands also said that you should copulate with us," but the women said, "Surely you are liars; go away; take the food out

Reprinted from Alexander M. Stephan, "Hopi Tales,"* Journal of American Folklore *42 (1929): 34–35.

to the fields, and do not speak so foolish." But the Hehe'ya had loitered so long that the men in the field were growing impatient and began to call to them to hasten their return. The cunning Hehe'ya expected this, so they said to the women, "Surely we are speaking truth, but if you do not believe us, listen to your husbands." So the women listened and sure enough they heard the men calling from the fields, *"I'ich chova!"*, and being thus convinced they yielded themselves to the Hehe'ya, who gave no more thought to carrying the food for the field workers. After a while the Hüi'ki came in to the village and, discovering the trick that had been put upon them, they lashed the Hehe'ya with yucca and drove them away.

PART TWO

GAY AMERICAN INDIANS TODAY

LIVING THE SPIRIT

M. OWLFEATHER

SHOSHONE-METIS/CREE

CHILDREN OF GRANDMOTHER MOON

Grandmother Moon comes slowly
   over the eastern hills.
Chanting a song, a song of a lost age,
   its meaning a mystery.
She comes dressed in orange calico.
Her hair wrapped in otter fur.
Her moccasins made of soft deer skin.
No one hears as she makes her journey
   to her lodge in the west.
Before her goes the owl, flying by night.
Singing, "Hush, respect your grandmother
   She is old and knows many things.
   Say nothing as she passes."
Sometimes she sends owl out, to warn her people
   of someone about to die.
He chants a verse, three times
   for three nights,
   before it happens.
This makes her very sad, her people are few.
You can tell she weeps
   because you find
   Her tears
On the grass and trees when she's gone.

The reservation where I live is a harsh place, situated on a high plateau valley in the west. Most people wonder why anyone would want to live here. The temperature ranges from one hundred de-

Buffalo Spirit, 18x24, tempera on bristol, 1982.
Joe Lawrence Lembo.

grees in the summer to forty below in the winter. Life is indeed hard. It takes a certain kind of person, or people, to call this place "home." My people have lived in this place for many, many generations and consider it more than home; it is the place from where we come and to where we return. It is our mother and our special place in the world.

Many people ask me, "Why do you stay here? You have a good education, you have traveled the world and lived in many places, many different lives, so why return? There is no work here, little or no pride; there is depression, desolation, no hope. And for a person such as you, a gay Indian, what is there for you here, except perhaps criticism and humiliation?"

All of the above is true. But still I am here and surviving. I have a supportive group of friends, Indian and non-Indian, gay and straight. I hide my lifestyle and interests from no one. I participate in Indian traditional dances and religion. In a small town and in a tribal group of four thousand people nothing is hidden.

I returned to the reservation four years ago. I still remember a time when I vowed that I would never return. But despite all the situations listed above, the fact remains that I did return because there is something here that exists for an Indian person nowhere else: the sense of belonging, of family and of the land. You are not only a person, alone, but an extension of a family and a group of people, a "tribe," that has existed before the written word and history. It is a unique place and people, something that non-Indians cannot really imagine or feel. True, the culture is shattered, broken . . . and the people's lifestyle is in tatters and perhaps even still in culture shock to some degree. After all, my great-grandfather and great-grandmother saw the last of the buffalo killed. A lifestyle they knew and loved, with the rigors of moving camp and living in tipis, going anywhere they pleased, was destroyed.

Indian life and existence today is a paradox of the old and new. Christian beliefs are held along with native traditions. Western lifestyles are combined with traditional Indian lifestyles, and a number of people get hopelessly lost. Not respecting themselves or anyone else, some get angry, some get drunk, and some deny the Indian culture or anything Indian because they think it is useless in this present day and age.

No wonder a young man of nineteen years that I know and sleep with sometimes says to me, "I don't want to have people call me a queer or a faggot, but I want to be with you," or that I have a longstanding married lover who throws rocks at my window when the moon is full, wanting me to come out and play. He says, "I'm married, but I have always loved you and always will." Gay and bisexual Indian men and women are no different from anyone else in their fear of criticism. But I think it is more intense within a tribal structure, because our traditional way of correcting behavior is public chastisement and ridicule. And today, the view of the gay Indian man or woman has been twisted to fit the mix of Christian and Indian beliefs in contemporary tribal culture.

In the old days, during life on the plains, the people respected each other's vision. Berdaches had an integral place in the rigors and lifestyle of the tribe. The way they were viewed was not the same as the contemporary Indian gay lifestyle and consciousness that we have now—they were not fighting for a place in society and to be accepted by that society. They already had a place, a very special and sacred place. They were the people who gave sacred names, cut down the Sun Dance pole, and foretold future events. They were renowned for their bead and quillwork and hide-tanning abilities and fancy dress. (Not all berdaches dressed in women's clothes; it depended on their vision.) It was considered good luck to have a berdache on a war party or on a horse-stealing raid. If a man wanted to, and had the ability to take a second or third wife, many times a man of the berdache vision would be chosen.

But all this changed with the coming of the reservation period in Indian history and the systematic crushing of all things Indian. The berdache visionaries were one of the outstanding targets, especially those who dressed and had the mannerisms of the opposite sex. (Some of these men were married to women, but maintained the dress of their vision.) The last record of a berdache on my reservation was in the early 1900s.

You must understand that in the period of 1880 to 1910, if you were found or caught practicing Indian beliefs or dress, you could be jailed. Even if an Indian man wore his hair long, which was his pride, he could be jailed and punished. The great summer Sun

Dance was suppressed. In one district of my reservation the dance was stopped by cutting down the Sun Dance pole in the midst of the ceremony. In another instance, the dance was held on a Mormon rancher's property where the government had no jurisdiction. So it was with little wonder that the vision of the berdache was forgotten or suppressed to the point that it was no longer mentioned and barely remembered. When it was mentioned, it was with shame and scorn, due to the influence of Christianity on Indian people. It is into this type of belief system and society that gay Indian men and women are born today.

On my reservation, it is traditional for the firstborn of a generation to live and be raised by the grandparents. They are called the "old peoples' children," and they are taught the knowledge, traditions, songs, and lifeways of the tribe. Usually these people either become respected members of their community and tribe or turn out to be totally useless!

I was raised in this manner and lived a wonderful childhood. I was raised by my grandmother in a little one-room cabin that she and my great-uncle built in the 1920s. We had a wire strung for drying meat and hanging dish towels and clothing. In the center of the room we had a big round oak table covered with oilcloth. My grandmother's friends would come to visit and have coffee. Sometimes my great-aunts or great-uncles could come. I always knew my place, but would sometimes sit with them and drink coffee with lots of sugar and canned milk in it. I always enjoyed these visits and still feel more comfortable with Indian elders than with people my own age. I lived through their tales and my grandmother's own stories. In the winter she would tell "coyote stories." I felt very secure hearing those stories of our family and tribe and would listen very intently after the fire had burned down and everyone was bedded down for the night. The winter nights were wonderful when those stories were told, with the snow blowing around the edges of the cabin.

Our life was very simple by non-Indian standards. In the mornings when I was older I would chop wood and pump water—those would be my chores at the start of each day. After breakfast, which was either oatmeal or pancakes, my sister and I would venture forth to greet the day and many adventures.

My relationships with children my age were limited. Besides my sister and several cousins, I had very few young friends. Even at an early age I was attracted to members of my own sex. I was dreaming in my childhood. I knew that I was different in my attraction to other boys and men. I always had this dream in which a bearded man would open his arms to me and say "Come." When I was eight years old, I experienced my vision and found out how truly different I was.

It was during a hot, dry, and dusty Idaho summer, when I was eleven, that I had my first real contact with another male. I had more freedom then. I had both a pony and a red bicycle. With those possessions my circle of friends widened. I met a boy who lived a few blocks down from my grandmother's cabin. He was a local white boy some years older than myself. I admired his independent and cocksure ways. He seemed to be everything that I was not: good in sports and, above all, sure of himself in every situation. He had tousled brown curly hair and was somewhat stocky. He became my hero in the eye of my budding desire.

The local boys our age frequented several well-known swimming holes on the reservation. We always picked one that was well secluded with overhanging trees and green grass on the banks. One day toward the end of summer—on the kind of day when the light is hazy and diffused and the air is barely moving and heavy to breathe—my friend and I decided to have an impromptu swim before returning home. The water was cool and clear as we dove in. I came up from under the water first. He came up right behind me and reached around and into my shorts (we always swam in our undershorts). I noticed that he was hard, as he rubbed against my backside. As his hands reached around me . . . I became aroused and hard, too. It felt good and right, like something that was supposed to be. I knew then that this is what I had been waiting for and I have never looked back since.

After that summer and after many more rendezvous, my friend moved away. I was dumbstruck. I had found a companion, someone to share with and be my friend, closer than a brother or a buddy. But then he was gone. My young heart experienced for the first time the loneliness and the ache of missing someone that you love. Since that time I have found many more boys and men of all races in many different cities and countries and situations. But of course, there is no time like the first time. It is something that is burned in my memory, like those hot Idaho August days, so long ago.

It is unfortunate that among today's gay Indians the great tradition and vision of the old-time berdache has been suppressed and is nearly dead. Gay Indians today grow up knowing that they are different, act in a different way, and perceive things in a different light from other Indians. They know these things, but sometimes are afraid to act or acknowledge their gayness. If they do, they try to accept and emulate the only alternative lifestyle offered to them, that of the current gay society of bars, baths, and, until recently, numerous sex partners. It is no wonder that many succumb to alcohol or drug addiction and early death. Today I see so many of my Indian brothers and sisters with the same vision living a life that is damaging to themselves, denying or fighting against what they really are. I see and know many gay Indians on the reservation and elsewhere that think along the following lines: "It's okay for you to go to bed with me. I will talk to you in bars or when I want to fuck. But don't come around me in Indian society, at pow-wows, or other tribal functions. I don't want our people to know. Nobody knows my secret but everyone knows what you are and what you like to do."

To escape this kind of thinking and the oppressive lifestyle that gay Indians are often forced to live on the reservations, many go to the city and follow the way of the non-Indian gay society—taking up the latest trends in fashion, carrying on in the bars, or dancing the night away in discos and after-hours clubs and, of course, having sex, lots of it. I followed this way myself for many years, but in the end I became tired of it all. Deep inside I knew that, as an Indian, something else was needed—something more than poppers, drugs, booze, fashion, restaurants, bars, gay shops, cock rings, leather, drag, and the latest dance hits—especially for a person of substance and especially for an Indian person. Most Indian people, gay or straight, have been instilled with a respect for all things, a love for the earth and all things living. The current gay lifestyle, although it is an up-front gay existence, is not an Indian way. Most gay Indians become lost in it, not only to themselves but to their cultures, tribes, and sometimes families as well.

In the past ten years, however, efforts have been made by gay Indians who live in the cities to found support groups and social organizations for urban gay Indians as well as those across the country on reservations and in other rural areas. They are to be commended. Organizations such as Gay American Indians of San Francisco and the Native Cultural Society of Vancouver, British Columbia, are at least there to provide the positive statement and support needed by so many gay Indians. They exist to say, *"We are here, we exist, we are INDIAN and we are GAY!!"* That is very important, not only to those in the cities but also to the gay Indian living on the reservation. Many live in such isolation that they cannot react to other gay Indian people in a positive way and are afraid to associate with other gay Indians because of social ostracism or criticism.

In the old days, groups of berdaches lived on the outer edge of the camp. They lived together in a tipi or a group of tipis that were usually the best made and decorated in camp. The old-time berdaches had a pride in their possessions and in themselves. They knew who they were and what place they had in Plains Indian society.

I believe this is exactly what needs to happen again with gay Indians today. There is a need to take pride in one's self and to respect other gay Indian people. There is a need for a resurgence of that old pride and knowledge of place. Traditions need to be researched and revived. If traditions have been lost, then new ones should be borrowed from other tribes to create groups or societies for gay Indians that would function in the present. An example of this is the contemporary pow-wow that takes elements from many tribal groups and combines them into an exercise in modern Indian tradition and social structure.

I am not saying that we should all go "back to the blanket" or return to the reservation. But somehow, there should be a blending of the old with the new, to develop more within ourselves and our consciousness—as a people living on the "outer edge," possessing a unique and valid vision and a place in the history and contemporary lifestyle of our country.

When you are born into this world, you reach for either a bow and quiver, which is blessed and protected by the Sun, our Grandfather, or you reach for an awl and sewing bag, which is blessed by the Moon, our Grandmother. From that time on you will follow that vision and be blessed.

—Traditional Indian belief and teaching

ERNA PAHE

NAVAJO

SPEAKING UP

Where did you grow up?

I was born on the Apache reservation and lived there until I was about six, because my mom and dad worked at the boarding school. Then we moved to Phoenix and lived there a couple years. I graduated from high school in Flagstaff, Arizona. After a couple years in college, I moved back to the reservation (Window Rock, Arizona) until I was about twenty-three—365 days a year on the reservation. I left when my son was just a baby and came to California and have lived here for fourteen years now.

Where did you go to college?

Cochise College in Douglas [Arizona].

It was a small college and I was the only Indian. That gave me kind of a separate feeling, but it was a good feeling, too. It was, "Oh, a *real* Indian?" I didn't realize that was special. When you go to boarding school on the reservation you were no different from anybody else. It was a new thing for me, just finding out that there were people interested in your background. It was really a trip!

When you're raised on the reservation, you're very family-oriented. Even when we moved from Window Rock to Fort Defiance—only seven miles away—it was like a big tear, like really creating a division in the family.

Erna Pahe has served as Executive Director and President of Gay American Indians. She was interviewed by Will Roscoe on July 19, 1985.

After I came out here to California, the first time I went back people said, "Oh, where have you been?" "Oh, in California." "You're in California?" It's like the Wizard of Oz to them. When I first saw the ocean and heard the roar, it was the excitement of my life.

I didn't even know that Indian agencies existed for the first three or four years that I was here. It took me another couple years to understand the difference between "urbans" and "rurals." At home we didn't consider ourselves rural, but that's what we were. Out here I say I'm just Indian, but when you get closer into the politics of Sacramento they'll say, "Well, who do you represent? Urban or rural?" "What does that mean? We're all Indians so it shouldn't make any difference." But that's the division that constantly gets thrown at us. And it's true—they were working to keep us separated.

Did you have any kind of role models, you know, like the proverbial gym teacher?

When I went to college I thought my PE teacher was *it*—even though she had a boyfriend and was going to get married. That crush that you always have on your PE teachers . . . hey, I had it. I'm a witness!

How old were you when you came out?

I was about twenty-three or twenty-four.

Back home on the reservation, I knew the feeling that I was having. But being that close and being the youngest one of the family, I didn't have much of a chance to be an individualist, I guess.

It's not anything that's ever talked about. It's not dealt with. You're a member of the family, that's the priority. The chain of command in our family is real sturdy in that the oldest boy is more or less the father. So we all work real hard to make sure we don't do anything or say anything that is going to upset him.

In our tradition, we don't talk back to our elders, whether they're a few years older or ten or twelve years older. It's a respect that we're taught. They say, "I don't want to talk about it," you don't talk about it.

When I came out here I finally got that feeling that I had control over my own life and didn't have anybody else to answer to. So it was good for me, because when I did go back to the reservation I was ready to deal with "Hey, I'm just me. I'm the baby sister of the family, but I'm independent and I do have my life to live, whichever way I choose to live it."

Do you think that gay Navajo people have to leave the reservation to be able to come out?

I think they can be gay and still live there. A lot of it depends on the area that you're in. If you're way secluded, like in Snake Flats or Chinle, it isn't going to make any difference to anybody. If you get into Window Rock, which is the capital with a big population, and you have a lot more of the educated Indians who have lived in Flagstaff and heard the criticisms, there's quite a bit of discrimination. Not that I've necessarily felt it. It seems that way.

What are your positive memories of the reservation?

Well, what I think about the most is the opennness. When you wanted to get away there was a place to do it. There's accessibility where you can just go out and find an old shed to stay in—and you know you're not going to be bothered. And then, I miss the closeness of my family. Being able to call them up and say "Let's have a picnic this afternoon."

I do like the city in the sense that you have a lot of things you can do. You have access to all kinds of things without having to travel miles. When you need to go out and talk to people, you can always find someone that doesn't know you or doesn't know your family. Out home, everybody knows you.

Why do many Indians have a hard time accepting gay people?

In the past, there was very little talk about your personal life or personal feelings. The basic thing was our traditions—and not so much feelings. It took me until I got out of college and moved to this area before I started speaking up—"Well, yeah, I am gay"—after I had heard the word and realized its interpretations.

Even when I go back home now, and even though my family knows, we never talk about it. The spiritual way is always put as a priority . . . your personal side of life is a little different.

For the elders, that's the way it was in their home. So it's like a new idea. All of a sudden Indians are starting to speak up—and it's not all around politics. Now they see a new generation of kids coming up that are actually saying "This is the way I am, that's it"—where they were always real quiet and never were taught to speak with their heartfelt feelings unless it dealt with the whole tribe—what *our* people want.

But, you know, it's kind of like they've led us into it, too, saying "Speak up, speak up—say your piece." You can just see how excited they get as older people. It's a trip.

What are some of the things GAI has been doing to be active in the Indian community here in the Bay area?

One of the most positive things we've done is to be aware of other programs' problems. When their funds are being cut and what they really need is a whole bunch of Indians to go over there at city hall to speak up, they'll say "If you want people to come out, call GAI."

We're really getting into the community. We're getting involved in the alcoholism programs, in urban Indian health, the Indian Center, all these agencies. If they need people there, our community can come together. Just going out and fighting and supporting these agencies, even though we never utilize the program, is what I think has developed GAI recently. And because we do it in a positive way.

This is something that, for the Indian agencies, has been many years coming. Five, six years ago you would have said "Oh, this agency doesn't ever go to the same meetings as this agency"—because of personality conflicts or whatever. But now communities are coming together and they all are going after things that are very positive. I think that's what's really helped.

The other thing that I noticed that's real interesting is seeing elders like Sayoqah, who in the past kept herself as a spiritual leader, somebody that would always do the blessings, now coming up and sitting on our board of directors. The elders are speaking up, reaffirming that traditional attitude. It's putting the whole, traditional, older philosophies back into the thinking that we're doing now.

I think that the Indian community is making a big move. Randy Burns put it real good a couple years ago, saying that it's a sleeping giant waking up and coming to life. Indians have sat back so many years and seen all these other minority groups get their way and say "Geez, how did they do it?" It's taken more generations for us to get to where we're at right now. But we're really becoming vocal. We're getting involved in legislative things coming out of Washington—mental health, urban Indian health, and all this kind of stuff. We've found a tool now and that tool is speaking up.

Do you see connections between what gay Indians do today and the traditional roles they may have had in the past?

Because we're more vocal now, we're admired a lot more. The gay people that are fifty or sixty years old now are sitting back. And of course they're going to be a tad bit jealous, because we more or less had the guts to open up, where the way they lived in their time wasn't necessarily to open up or speak about what you were, but to act it and play it to the hilt. It was easier for them to just go in and start the fire and grind the corn and sit next to the women and laugh and joke—because it was actual hard work, they just sat there and constantly worked, and two hands are better than one. The women encouraged that input from the males, because they could see that they tried so hard. But they didn't have to say anything about it. They didn't ask questions and that person or individual didn't try to make their stand known. It was done very quietly.

Now the whole move is to be vocal and to tell everybody, "Hey, we want an equal share of this pie." When I'd say, "Oh, yeah, I'm chairperson on the board of directors of GAI," a lot of them did criticize me. They'd say "Well, you're out there, you're trying to be different. You're trying to say yes, you're an Indian, but you're trying to be a *different* Indian than the rest of us." So it took time for us to educate them and tell them.

But now that we're beginning to make a positive impact on society, and they're starting to see headlines—you know, about gay organizations or gay discrimination cases—all of a sudden it's just like another household word. They're even wanting to be more involved in the group—it's because they feel now that there's nothing wrong with me speaking out about the things I don't like. You know, even though I used to get teased when I was small, I went ahead and ground that corn and didn't say anything. But don't try that on me now!

Some people that I've known for seven, eight years are just now getting around to being honest. They have no qualms about saying, "Oh, you want to know something about gay Indians? We have a board member here that's affiliated with Gay American Indians." The straight Indian community is willing to give out that information now. They're really getting behind the gay Indians because it's a new issue, it's a new group of people that are really full of energy. That's what's tripping out the Indian community. They've been fighting the same people, and it doesn't seem like they're progressing anywhere. And here, all of a sudden, in the last three, four years GAI has surpassed what they've been attempting to do for ten years—getting involved in the politics of the local community. They come up to us and say "Oh, do you guys know anybody in the senator's office?"

Basically, we're playing the game of the government. They make cutbacks at Indian health clinics in order to give additional monies for, just using an example, AIDS. But how much of that research actually goes on on the reservation or in the Indian community?

What kind of role do you think gay Indians can play in politics today and in the community in general?

Politically, we will play a very neutral role. Right now you look in politics and you see the Democratic party, the Republican party. What we're doing is like taking those two entities and adding a third party. It's very people oriented, very mutual, very middle in trying to bring all the facets of the world together.

We're the one group of people that can really understand both cultures—as mothers, as females, as young girls versus fathers and men. You go out there into the straight world and it's really amazing the stereotypes. Men can do this and women can't do that. Or women can do this and men can't do that.

In our culture, in our little gay world, anybody can do anything. I mean, you find some very good mothers that are men. And you find very good fathers that are women. We can sympathize, we can really feel how the other sex feels. More so than the straight community. The straight community is so worried about staying within their little box and making sure that I look like a female when I'm out there, or that I really play the role of a male image.

I think that society is ready for that kind of atmosphere where we don't have to compete against each other over sexual orientation, or we don't have to feel like the men play a bigger role in society than women do. I think it's time for that neutralness, where people can understand just how to be people.

Why does GAI use just the word gay, instead of gay and lesbian?

That's a good one. It gets back to that division again. I've always advocated for the idea that "gay" meant more or less homosexual, whether you were female, whether you were male, whether you were black or white or whatever. I don't especially think that there's a distinction. Other people say "gay" reflects males, though. That's very hard for me to conceive, to understand. All gay people to us are all gay people—they're men and women.

What advice would you give to a young woman who is Indian and discovers she'd rather go on softball trips than to the prom?

The advice I most hope that young Indian women would have is to be patient. It's hard coming out—coming out to your family, being able to sit down and talk with them. It's something I've yet to do with my family. Yet I know they understand; we understand each other. But it's being patient.

I see a lot of young Indian girls and they come out and they're just gung-ho about it. Then the first time they go home, especially after being in an urban area where it's so free, you get discouraged real easy because of the simple fact that at home we don't talk like that. It's just kind of understood. So they get all gung-ho, and they expect a lot of changes in a short period of time, and you can't expect that, especially of your family. Patience is probably the most important thing.

Then as you go through these different types of relationships—I imagine I'll go through a few more in my life—but that's part of life, meeting people. The first time I fell in love with the first woman and it didn't work out, it about tore my heart out. I thought, "Why am I doing this to myself?" It takes being patient and searching and not expecting too much out of the gay life, because it's just as hard as straight life, if not a little bit harder.

There's women that have children that are coming out now. With them you have to be very patient. Bringing them up with the idea that there isn't anything wrong with it. As my son goes out now with his teenage girlfriends, I can imagine the things he goes through to explain the lifestyle in our home. He's had the neighbor kids tease him and talk to him about dykes and come home saying "What does 'dykes' mean, Mom?" Bringing him up to not be bitter about it. That all falls into that patience. You have to be very, very patient.

And especially the personalities of gay people. It seems to be that gay people are a lot more intense about life in general. They're a lot more keen on feelings, other peoples' feelings. I don't know why that is but it just seems that way to me.

There's a lot of caring in gay people that is toward all lifestyles, from children all the way up to grandparents. Society is getting used to it now because of this sensitivity. I think it might wear off after a while—we'll get everybody thinking like us. Even dealing in politics, we're a lot more aware of everything—how it is to go through parenthood, how it is to have babies—more so than anybody else. Yeah, we are special, because we're able to deal with all of life in general. It's very special.

DEBRA S. O'GARA
TLINGIT

GRANDPA'S LITTLE GIRL

I awoke and the sun was already up and I could hear the hustle and bustle of the village outside my window. Then I remembered my plans to go berry picking. It was our second day off and they said there wouldn't be fish in for another day at least. It's like a long vacation to us cannery workers after working twelve to sixteen hours a day for several weeks.

After I finished my chores and my room was all picked up, I went downstairs to the store, the hub of the village. It was only midmorning but the store was already full with families stocking up on groceries for fish camp, buying extra parts to repair boat motors and nets, picking out a new warm shirt or mailing letters to relatives. There were some who were just standing about visiting, catching up on news or just plain gossiping.

I went into the post office, a tiny little office with a big picture window looking out on the river, to say good morning to my grandfather. I waited until he finished waiting on a customer. I love to watch him when he is working. He is a very tall man who knows just about everyone and everyone knows him. He is very respected and is sought out for advice not just by people here in Mountain Village but from all over the area. I told him what I was planning for the day and that I would be back in time to fix his dinner. He sent me on my way but only after he made me promise to make blueberry pies tonight with the berries I will bring back. Blueberry pie is his favorite; mine, too.

I went looking for my friends so we could find a boat to go upriver where the berries are bigger and riper. The group was down behind the warehouse near the fuel tanks, talking very fast and excitedly as I approached. They were all older than I was, but that's not unusual. They were speaking in Eskimo when I joined them, but they switched over to half English so that I could understand and join in better.

This was my third summer at Mountain, and I'm slowly starting to understand the language. Lenore had been teaching me this year and I was learning faster.

"Why are you all so excited?" I asked.

"There is a plane coming in the morning to pick up firefighters," Alex told me. "Everyone is planning on going. Jimmy, Mike, and Pat have gone out before," he said. "And when they pick you up they take you to wherever the fires are. You don't know where, but you get to travel away for a week or so and come back with lots of money."

I wasn't aware that girls didn't usually go or that it was dangerous. Lenore had gone the year before, and she told me that there were only three other girls that went from our whole area. But I wanted to go. Lenore was going, and most of our friends, who were mostly boys, were going. Besides, it sounded like a lot of fun and I wasn't going to miss out.

I ran up to my aunt's house and burst in the door, full of excitement and the prospects of adventure. She said, "Why do you want to go fight fires? It's dirty and hard, dangerous work. Besides, you'll just end up cooking and not make as much money as you think." She tried to dissuade me. "It's not proper for a girl of thirteen years to go off someplace unknown to do men's work." But she said that the decision was not hers and that I would have to ask my grandfather.

I had to convince him that I should go and that it would be a wonderful experience for me. But he also didn't think I should go. It was too dangerous. He kept saying "Girls don't do men's work. Firefighting is men's work, and besides, what would people think if my granddaughter was off gallivanting around somewhere, who knows where?"

"Grandpa, I don't care what other people are going to think, and I won't be gallivanting around. I'll be working. You've seen me work, and you know I can do it." We kept going around and around, but he wasn't giving in, and I wasn't giving up.

Finally, when we had both seemed to reach total exasperation with each other, I blurted out at him, "If I were your grandson, you wouldn't hesitate a minute to give me permission to go!"

My words and bluntness shocked us both; I was not accustomed to being so forward with him. I thought to myself, "Now I've really blown it. Now he'll never let me go." But he recovered from his surprise at my words and agreed with me. "If you were a boy, my grandson, I wouldn't hesitate to let you go." He would see it as a valuable adventure of life, and he had to admit, not just to me but to himself, that he was saying "No, you can't" based solely on me being a girl. He realized that maybe that wasn't right. "If you really want to go, then I think you should."

The excitement of the new adventure caught him, almost as much as it already had me, as I asked him what I should pack and what I would need. While we were making a list of things that I had and things I would need to get, he began remembering back to when he went off to fight fires as a young man.

He said the most important item I would need was a good, sturdy pair of warm boots. If I got my feet wet, then I would catch a chill that could last for days no matter how much I bundled up. And rain gear with good warm, wool clothes for under the rain gear. He explained to me that a firefighting crew could be on the move for up to a week to keep up with the fire. If anyone got wet, there would be no time to stop to dry out. If this happened, it could prove to be a cold, miserable, awful week.

While we walked through the store looking for just the right boots, he was telling me stories of the few firefighting trips he had gone on to pick up extra money. Once he was gone for ten whole days and never saw the fire. He was on the backup crew on standby in case the fire broke through the fire lines. He just saw an awful lot of smoke.

Another time he went and didn't even lie down to rest for two and a half days. That's when he was glad he had a good sleeping bag to crawl into, even though it was for a very short time. On that note we walked over to the sleeping bags and picked out a good, warm, lightweight one.

My grandfather and I were relating on a new level that was very different. I was very excited about going and he was excited for me. He joked with me and at the same time warned me.

Warned me that the bosses could be tough, and that I would have to be tough back. I would have to prove to them, like I had to him, that I was very capable for the job. He said this with confidence in his voice, as if he believed as much as I did that, given half the chance, I could do the job.

My relationship with my grandfather was never the same again. I was no longer his little girl needing to be taken care of but a person in my own right.

That night I couldn't sleep. What will I be doing? Where are the fires? How long will we be gone? Will I have to convince the fire bosses that I hate to cook and will be much better with a shovel? "You bet I will," I think to myself. I can do that, though. If I can convince my grandfather, then I can convince anyone. Girls can go firefighting, too!

The plane came and took the first load away. I got my name on the list for the second load. The plane would be back that evening and I was ready. But it never came back. It must have gotten enough workers for the crews from the other villages. My bag stayed packed for five days, but the plane never came back.

It didn't matter, though. I had achieved something much more important. I knew I could do anything I wanted—I just needed to know how to move the obstacles out of the way.

A boatload of salmon came in early the next morning, and we all went back to work, and I made some more money and learned some more Eskimo words.

KIERAN PRATHER/JERRY

HUPA

BECOMING INDIAN

"I come from a medicine family. My aunt is spiritual leader of the tribe now."

The California volume of the *Handbook of North American Indians* is opened to a photograph taken in the 1880s, a picture of Captain John, a shaman of the Hupa tribe. Jerry points to the deerskin wrap, to the stone-bladed thrusting spear, to the necklace of dentalium shells. He explains the sweathouse low to the ground behind the posed Indian and describes its use and design.

Jerry now talks about the White Deerskin Dance, the main ceremony of the Hupa religion, about the albino deerskin that is valued for its rarity and for its symbolism. He explains that the celebration lasts for seven days and that different dances are involved: the Boat Dance, the Crazy Dance, and, of course, the White Deerskin Dance. There is a break of ten days, then the ceremonies close with the ten-day-long Jump Dance. He describes the ritual garments that are used with the dancing: the buckskin aprons, the dentalium-shell necklaces, the abalone pendants—and the treasured white deerskin.

He turns to another page in the book on Indian history: a 1902 photo shows a woman pouring water into a basket of acorn meal. Jerry tells of "calling the acorns" and talks about fasting and the ritual eating. He mentions other customs, emphasizing that the traditions remain the same as in his grandfather's time, as in the time of Captain John and before.

Having described some of the ceremonies, Jerry attempts to explain about a medicine family, about spiritual leadership.

Based on interviews with Jerry, a member of the Hupa tribe, from September 1985 to October 1986.

Hulleah Tsinhnahjinnie.

"My aunt is the spiritual leader of the tribe now. Before her, it was my great-uncle, then it was my great-grandmother. But it's more than family. The training, the learning of the rituals—it has to be somebody who knows all those things. There are the chants, the practice of the healing art, the ceremonies. It doesn't always go in a direct family line. . . . Part of it is who wants to do it." Jerry pauses, seeking other ways to show how leadership is both inherited and not inherited, how a spiritual force is related to material substance.

The Hupa reservation is located in the extreme northwest corner of California, a narrow, six-mile stretch of land along the Trinity River. For centuries the Hupa Indians have occupied this valley, isolated from other cultures, building their tiny villages along the banks of the river. White trappers wandered onto their land in the early 1800s but did not stay; the first attempts at white settlement came with the discovery of gold along the Trinity River in the 1850s (Wallace 1978:164–79).

This land was remote and, once the gold mines were bled dry, was deemed worthless by white men. So when Congress established the Hoopa Valley Indian Reservation in 1864, it set aside most of the existing Hupa territory for the Indians. Thus the Hupa people stayed in their valley, and their uninterrupted occupancy insured the survival of religious practices and values. The Hupa did not suffer the disintegration that afflicted most other tribes. In 1862 the census placed the Hupa population at 1,000; in 1962 the population was counted as 992.

Hupa culture is materialistic, with power and social status directly related to wealth. The political leader is likely to be the richest man in the village; social importance is measured by association with the wealthy members of society. Today wealth might include money and property, but still of importance are the traditional heirlooms: the obsidian-bladed spears, the ornaments made of dentalium shells, the woodpecker-scalp headbands, and the albino deerskins.

At the same time, the Hupa tradition possesses a rich spiritual element. The shaman has historically held a powerful position within the tribe, both as leader in religious ceremony and one who practices the healing art. Belief in good and evil is clear-cut for the Hupas, with black magic being the power to inflict pain and harm and white magic the art of healing.

Religious ceremonies are held at various times during the year, but most important is the White Deerskin Dance, which begins on the first day of the full moon in September every other year. For a period of seven days, all life focuses on this celebration. Prayers and dances recount the beginnings of the Hupa tribe. The acorn, the traditional food staple of the Hupas, is a frequently used symbol, signifying the belief that the dance will insure good crops and a plentiful harvest. The spiritual leader controls the ceremony, as a "presence" whose power validates the ritual actions and as the director of activities involving participation by other members of the tribe.

Jerry was born on the Hoopa Valley Reservation in 1949 and lived there until he was thirteen. By that time the reservation had a white population whose lives were integrated with those of the Indians. "I went to school with white kids and they were my friends just like Indians were. I knew I was Indian, of course, but that didn't make any difference. I didn't feel special." He had the same attitude about his own culture. "I knew we were a medicine family, but that wasn't important. The ceremonies and things were part of the usual lifestyle. It was just what we did."

At thirteen Jerry began his tour of foster homes away from the reservation. In Eureka, Arcata, and Blue Lake, he lived the lives of the white families he stayed with. Being an Indian was even less important. He returned to the reservation at the age of seventeen, but Hoopa Valley was no longer home to him, and he did not feel comfortable there. After a few months he set out on his own, moving to San Francisco. He chose a nontraditional occupation, becoming a student at a cosmetology school.

San Francisco in the late 1960s became for Jerry what it was for so many others. A stranger on the reservation where he had been born, he now forged links with others who had also experienced alienation. In San Francisco Jerry found acceptance and identity.

"I first experienced drugs at the school. They were easy to get; a lot of people used them. Also, it was my friends at school who introduced me to other people who were into drugs, who were really wild."

The use of drugs, at first an experiment with friends, became his principal recreation and then his main goal. And for a gay teenager into drugs, street prostitution is an inevitability. "I was fascinated by these people, and I spent lots of time with them. I began to do the things they did, and I got more daring. That's when I started hustling and living the street life. Then I started doing drag. Hustling was easier because you could get into bars in drag when you couldn't otherwise."

The drugs got heavier and the sex became more important; he dropped out of school. But life seemed good because there were always johns who took a fancy to the young Indian, always somebody willing to support him and his lifestyle.

"The johns were always there. It didn't matter who it was, as long as he had money. You stayed awhile, then moved on. You had to move around, go get the next one. You couldn't stay too long or let the person get too close. Only once did I let a man get really close to me."

At first, during those years, Jerry made periodic visits back to the reservation, but they were uncomfortable and brief. The distance between his two cultures had grown immense. It wasn't long before he stopped making those trips altogether.

Hustling did not always net the needed income for an established drug habit. Jerry, like many others, supplemented with petty thievery, robbery, forgery, and fraud. Surprised during a burglary in 1974, Jerry stabbed a policeman. When the man later died, Jerry was convicted of murder and sentenced to life imprisonment.

Every life has its unexpected miracles, and Jerry's most dramatic one came three years later. New evidence—presented, amazingly, by the policeman's widow—proved that the death had not been the result of wounds inflicted during the robbery. "Murder" became "assault," and punishment was reduced to time already served. Jerry was suddenly set free. But in less than three months he was arrested again and convicted of money-order fraud. He spent the next two years in the federal correctional institution on Terminal Island.

When he was released from prison this second time, for a short period he went back to the drugs, back to the streets. But it could not last. In the spring of 1980, in Los Angeles, Jerry reached "bottom," that time of decision when even though he couldn't imagine living any other way, he knew he couldn't continue this way. For Jerry, this was the first step in reclaiming his Indian life.

"My boyfriend and I came down here from San Luis Obispo. We decided to go into detox together. Then I got separated from him, but I went into a recovery house anyway. I didn't know what else to do."

A month after entry into his recovery program, Jerry had to get a job, a necessary step in the rehabilitation process. He began working with an Indian social service center in a suburb of Los Angeles. After six months he transferred to the United American Indian Involvement crisis center on skid row. At a time when he was building his own self-assurance and identity, he became a counselor for other urban Indians who had also "failed."

The nature of the problems Jerry dealt with each day were varied: economic difficulties, problems with police and parole boards, alcoholism and drug addiction, the need for a job or a place to stay, connecting runaway youths with their families and tribes, and so on. But always there was contact with his people, and whether he wanted it or not, there was contact with the culture he once ran from.

"I didn't take the job because it meant working with Indians. I wanted to do counseling, and this was a job I could get. I would have taken a job at a different place if there was one. But I was working with Indians, and I learned from that."

Jerry's transition was slow but steady. Free time that used to be spent watching television was now spent developing an old hobby: making Indian jewelry. Occasional attendance at Indian powwows became regular attendance once a month. More and more, time away from work was spent with friends who were Indian. Indians were not only clients but also brothers.

In the early 1980s Jerry returned to the reservation for the first time in ten years, testing the waters for a reunion with his family. It was successful beyond his hopes, especially the important visit with his aunt, the tribe's spiritual leader.

"We sat on her porch, just exchanging news, and she talked like I had never been away. It was like I had been in touch the whole time. She took it for granted that I would come back for the next White Deerskin Dance"

Jerry did return for the dance the following September, and he was given duties as a member of a medicine family, a relative of the shaman who led the ceremony. He was happy to participate and to fulfill these obligations. At long last he was coming home.

Back in Los Angeles, he wondered where he wanted to be. "I like what I'm doing here, but I really liked being back at the reservation. People in my family asked me to come back, they said they would help me get a job. If not back on the reservation, maybe in Eureka or one of the towns nearby." What amazed Jerry the most was that now he had a choice. His participation in the White Deerskin Dance and the invitation to come back were proof of acceptance that he had not felt at Hoopa since he was thirteen.

What of being gay?

"I guess it is a problem for some Indians with other tribes. I read about gay Indians and their problems of acceptance. But it's not that way for me. When I accepted myself, I found acceptance with my people. It's how you carry yourself. My clients and the people I work with know I am gay, and it doesn't make any difference. It stopped being a struggle when I stopped struggling with it.

"There are gay men who live on the reservation, and they lead happy lives. Your sexual life is your own business. If you take an active part in the life of the reservation, if you give input and show you care, you will be accepted. What matters is being a Hupa Indian."

Jerry accepts his gayness as an essential part of his personality rather than using it as a tool to manipulate others. In making peace with himself, he is better able to break down the barriers he has built between his cultural heritage and himself.

"I got in touch with a part of me that I had been denying. A part I couldn't see. Now I see it . . . and feel it.

"I'm not alone really. Guys go off, and nobody knows anything about them for years. Then they show up again, start going to powwows. In a little while they even begin dancing.

"That's what the reservation is for me now. Like a support group, I guess. But it's more than that. It's a spiritual source. . . . It's where I get strength."

In the spring of 1976 Jerry was called back to the reservation because of a serious illness in the family. He thought this might be the time to return for good. But while he did find growing acceptance with his family and old friends, he did not stay.

"There wasn't any work for me. There were a few possibilities, but they didn't work out. I even tried the towns near the reservation, but there wasn't anything.

"But my feelings haven't changed at all. I know that I will move back there someday. I spent a lot of time visiting and talking with people. I know that's where I want to be."

Today Jerry lives in Reno, working again as a counselor in an Indian alcoholism rehabilitation center. This time he interviewed for the job because he wanted to work with Indians.

"I feel I have something to offer them. The important thing is for them to identify with me because I am an alcoholic. But I think it is important that I am also an Indian, and I know what experiences Indians in urban areas can have. I know, and I care."

Jerry has spent much time reading books about Indian history and culture, especially works that focus on religion and mysticism. That has led to his own writing; he creates stories that reflect his own experiences, thoughts, and feelings, yet he places in them the symbols and framework of an Indian mystic tradition. This very personal experience is the latest step in completing the circle back to his Indian beginnings.

A poem written in honor of Jerry's great-uncle, who was spiritual leader of the Hupa tribe until his death in 1982, summarizes in a few lines the truth behind Jerry's own transformation:

To you, my people, remember that everything was given to you.
Remember the laws, the customs and the dances.
Remember to respect one another, then as always, disease,
Sickness and ill-feelings will blow out to sea.
Upon the strength of our prayers, upon you, O wind,
Cleanse our hearts and our homes.

Born on the Hoopa reservation, carried on official Hupa rosters all of his life, Jerry is, at last, becoming a Hupa Indian.

Postscript: In June 1987, Jerry moved back to Hoopa, where he manages the Indian Child Welfare Office.

LAWRENCE WILLIAM O'CONNOR

WINNEBAGO

A NATIONAL DISGRACE

The AIDS crisis facing gay men reminds me of a similar situation the original people of America encountered. Although American Indians have survived, at the turn of the century we were referred to as the "vanishing Americans." The Indians occupied land white people wanted, and the whites did everything possible to remove them from their land. Disease, decay, and alcoholism were introduced among the native people. Cheating and stealing took place on a grand scale. Every major treaty—even those promised as long as the grass grows and rivers flow—was broken. The buffalo were exterminated and an entire way of life ended. Genocide was practiced by the U.S. military. The first Americans' native land became their graveyard.

The white man knew no shame and became the so-called savages they were destined to civilize. In the end, the greatest tragedy for the American Indian is that the white man wrote the books, printed the newspapers, and produced the John Wayne movies. They were able to re-create history to fit their own image. The vast majority of Native Americans perished not from the white man's guns or starvation but from their sicknesses.

AIDS is a disease that essentially weakens the body's immune system to fight off disease and infection, eventually resulting in death. Like AIDS victims, the Indians had very weak immune systems. They had no immunity to European diseases such as smallpox, cholera, measles, and so forth. White people would visit an Indian camp and often the entire village would be coughing and sneezing, with a cold or worse, within a few days. For example, the Mandan nation along the upper Missouri River practically vanished overnight in 1837 when a smallpox epidemic struck. Of sixteen hundred Mandans, only thirty-one were left. In 1847 the Cayuse of Oregon all but disappeared within a few weeks from measles brought in by missionaries.

Germ warfare was invented in America as a means of exterminating Indians. "Gifts" of smallpox-infested blankets were distributed to Chief Pontiac's people by the British commander Sir Jeffrey Amherst in 1763. Where today are the Narragansets, the Hidatsa, or Illinois Indians, as well as hundreds of other tribes that once stood tall and proud on this land before the onslaught of the white man's epidemics?

It was never important that Indians were perishing in such great numbers. The only good Indian was a dead Indian. Each time an Indian lost land a white person gained land. Even today reservation Indians receive the poorest health care and have the lowest standard of living, socially and economically, of any other Americans. American Indians have the highest rates of infant mortality, suicide, unemployment, alcoholism, and illiteracy. Indians still die of tuberculosis and other diseases non-Indians stopped dying from decades ago. The average life expectancy for an American Indian is twenty-five years below the national life expectancy of the average American.

Every week I watch or hear of gay men who die of AIDS. Over twenty thousand have died. Each of those twenty thousand was a human life, a dream, that is now gone forever. AIDS is not a gay disease! In reality, it originated among a heterosexual population in Africa years before spreading to gays. Our government displays the same lack of concern today as it did when Indians were vanishing. It angers me to realize that if any other segment of the population besides homosexuals was being ravaged by such a terrible disease, the response of the federal government, medical establishment, and media would be so much more positive and concerted in terms of funding, research, and public awareness.

President John F. Kennedy left us a challenge in his following statement about the American Indian.

> Before we can set out on the road to success, we have to know where we are going, and before we can know that, we must determine where we have been in the past. It seems a basic requirement

> to study the history of our Indian people. America has much to learn about the heritage of our American Indians. Only through this study can we as a nation do what must be done if our treatment of the American Indian is not to be marked down for all times as a national disgrace.

America also has the challenge of waking up to the seriousness of the AIDS situation. A great deal more needs to be done by nongay Americans, or this nation's treatment of AIDS victims will also be remembered for all times as a national disgrace. I hope a lesson can be learned from history.

BEN THE DANCER

YANKTON SIOUX

GAY AMERICAN INDIANS

The generosity that Indians have toward others is a fine attribute. They give when there is plenty and when there is little. This generosity has deep roots that extend back to pre-European tribal life and traditions. Many tribes were made up of smaller bands, which were the strength of the tribe. These bands were not just a group of individuals united for a common purpose but rather a whole working unit that allowed individuality while stressing unity and cooperation. This led individuals to feel that they belonged to a whole society instead of small family units. Individuals united for a common goal. From this came a strong feeling of a united identity.

An example of this can be seen in the manner the Lakota Indians raised their young. Instead of the child being in the care of two parents or a single mother, the child was looked after by many members of the family and by nonfamily members of the tribe. This can also be seen in the Lakota language. For instance, the word for father in Lakota is *Ate,* but the child also addressed his father's brothers as *Ate,* as well. The same applied to the mother of the child, who along with her sisters was called *Ina.* This extended family system still has a great influence on many Lakota. Because of this, many Indians feel their Indianness is something that envelops not only the individual but the whole community. It also introduces a larger meaning to the word family. All of this also applies to gay Indians, which this article is about.

Most Indians are quick to offer an open handshake, nod of the head, or playful punch in the arm to warm the heart and express joy—a joy that you are who you are and that they are glad to know you. But with the warmth there is a hardness, as well. Distilled from a foreign culture, this hardness creates hate and distrust toward things not understood or accepted.

In the Lakota language, the word *wakan* means things holy or mysterious. This word is used to describe many things, such as *Wakan Takan,* the Great Mysterious One, *Sunka Wakan,* the Great Mysterious Dog (a horse), or simply things *wakan,* which were not easily explainable. In traditional Lakota values, things that were not understood were called *wakan* and left alone.

Due to this, the Lakota were very tolerant toward things that intrigued and alarmed non-Indians. They had an open-minded policy of trying to understand things instead of putting them down immediately. The ways of the old were honorable and wise, but sadly less and less of this finesse is being passed down to the modern generation.

The Lakota, who are united by a common culture and language, are now being divided by American mainstream values, such as income, religion, rural versus urban life, and gayness.

Indian gays on the reservation are subjected to the same conservative morality as Indian gays off the reservation in American society. This creates intolerance and segregates Indians even more. This is very hard on the gay individual, because of the strong home and community pressures to conform and strong feelings of belonging to a tribe. The ways of the traditional Lakota are to accept things rather than to change them; to learn to work with things and try to live in peace with them. This does not mean total agreement with the gay lifestyle, but it does mean tolerance. In traditional values there is a definite place for gays. Even though this does little to shelter the modern gay lifestyle, it does give an important validity to homosexuality and, more important, a heritage to Indian gays.

For many Indian gays, like their heterosexual counterparts, their heritage is a stable source of support and well-being. It means that he or she belongs to a special minority, founded on common history, language, and traditions. These are all building blocks for a healthy society. When these building blocks are neglected, cultural development comes to a standstill and stagnates. This is when foreign values set in and create contradictions within the culture and its philosophy. In the case of Indian gays, it breeds intolerance and nonacceptance. This, combined with harsh reservation life, makes the Indian gay lifestyle hard to live.

Luckily, there are Indians fighting to keep Indian traditions and values strong. There are also gay Indians who blend their gay lifestyle with tradition and who have made a good place in American society for themselves and others.

PAULA GUNN ALLEN
LAGUNA PUEBLO/SIOUX

SELECTIONS FROM *RAVEN'S ROAD*

In the deepening light of late afternoon, Allie turned her car west on the freeway, sighing with relief. She had dropped Grace off after Maggie, and now she was alone, on her way home. She loved the light as it was now, transforming the bleak mesas and the dusty city into a blazing effulgence of radiance. The shadows on the west mesa were long and deep, and the trees that filled the valley and lined the river at its lowest point threw gold into the air, a gold that was met by the gold of the dying sun. There were thunderheads piled tall and brooding on the edges of the world, mumbling their incantations deep in their ripening bellies. An occasional flash of lightning darted from their purple sides, testing its power along the clay and sandstone of the ground. She was filled with the fierce exultation that always came over her when she swooped down from the heights of the east or west mesa, speeding toward the valley floor; from light into shadow she plummeted, falling into the purple and green of the bosque's welcoming embrace. At the Rio Grande exit she left the freeway and turned north, feeling the simple excitement she always felt at this turn, the anticipation, as her mind, her spirit, flew ahead of her, darting and dipping through the cottonwoods along the twisting curves of the west valley roads as she drove steadily toward home. "Eagle am I," she chanted quietly, her voice deep and rumbling in her chest. "An eagle I fly."

It was her own song, one she had gotten from an eagle. She had been out, in the mountains of Washington, had spent weeks out there in the wilds, alone and half wild herself. That was long ago,

These selections from the author's forthcoming novel have previously appeared in New America: A Review.

Hin-mut-toe-ta-li-ka-tsut (Thunder Clouds Going Over Mountains), 1983.
Hulleah Tsinhnahjinnie.

years. Before she had become what she was, while she was still becoming. She was in her twenties then, fresh out of the service. "I'm a free woman," she would say, laughing with sardonic humor at the absurdity of the statement. Even then she knew the difference between discharged and free. Indeed, she knew that no one got discharged from America.

But for those weeks in the hills, alone with herself and whatever creatures chose to speak with her, alone with the great waters, the vast skies, the incurable rain, the endless forests, she knew freedom. And when she spoke of it, she knew what she was saying.

She had joined the army young, because she had heard a strange thing, because she was restless and full of angry vitality,

Hin-mut and Idelia, 1983.
Hulleah Tsinhnahjinnie.

because it was better than reform school, her alternative option. She had finished school, if that was what that miserable place could be called, and, drunk with independence, had returned home, where she learned another kind of drunkenness.

Her parents were dead by then, dead of the despair that afflicted so many of the People, and she didn't miss them any more dead than she had alive. They had been lost to her long before their deaths.

Sent to boardingschool when she was very small, abducted more than sent, actually, by white government agents as so many were during the years between the last of the Indian wars and the Second World War, her life had been confined to institutional care, uncare, most of the time. She hardly remembered her parents, hardly knew them. She had spent some summers with them, just a few. The powers felt that it was best for the children to stay away from the Indian community as much as possible. If they had had their way, no Indian child would have returned home after they were stolen and placed in the jail for children, the concentration camp for infant prisoners of war until each had been so thoroughly brainwashed and whitewashed that there would be no Indian spirit or mind left in that Indian body; where they had not suffered much more than gross neglect, laced more or less sparingly with abuse, and liberally dosed with daily, hourly, fear and humiliation.

A few had died of grief, starvation, beatings, running away, food poisoning, infections that went untreated, but most had survived. Bitter with helplessness to be sure but alive, they went out into the great world to find their fortune and make their way. The mutilation of spirit they had undergone did not show, not in any obvious way. It was a peculiar mutilation, mutation, one that ensured that, for the most part, they would become the kind of Indian white propaganda had determined was the only kind there was: savage, bloodthirsty, broken, hostile, and abjectly in need of the white man's salvation, his mercy, his compassion, his friendship, his regard—which, they had been thoroughly, painstakingly trained to know, they could never really gain.

After her "graduation," as they called it—it simply meant they judged her sufficiently tamed to be let loose on the short tether they named reservation lands, equipped with her BIA card so she could be tracked wherever she might roam in that land of the free, that home of the braves who were dead and dying dying still—she had made her way back to Coyote, a tiny village in Oklahoma, where she moved in with her grandmother, grandfather, and assorted relatives.

Avid for excitement, she had started running with a fast crowd, had left the village for Oklahoma City where she hit the streets for a time—"stolen by Deer Woman," they used to say—and was arrested for prostitution. In jail she had made a few friends, several enemies, and when she had finally been hauled before the justice of the peace—a weasel-like little man who had food or something worse stuck disgustingly in his mustache—and he gave her a choice between the army and the penitentiary, or reform school if it turned out she insisted on proving that she was underage; she chose the army. At least there, she reasoned, she would get paid. She could still party, drink and dance and raise hell. As for the danger—it was not part of her experience to worry about it. Danger and life were, to her, part and parcel of the same thing. "You gets what you pays for," she would say, and "I'm too broke to pay for much."

But what really decided her was something she had heard. She had been at a stomp dance in some Choctaw village, and late in the night she had taken her blanket to a place near some trees, away from the dance grounds. She had spread it out and lay down, prepared to sleep. But she could hear some women talking, low, somewhere near, so she got up to investigate. They heard her coming and called out to her to join them, and she did. Then they went back to their conversation. She couldn't see their features clearly in the dark, but she knew they were pretty old from their voices and the way they held themselves, so still, so quiet. They were talking about a strange thing that was coming, one of them had seen it when she had been out praying in the hills, the low, leafy mountains of eastern Oklahoma and Arkansas. There were long pauses between the sentences they exchanged.

"I'm not sure what it was," one was saying. "It looked like the ground opened up and the thunders emerged. The sky cracked open as well. There was light, oh, the light, climbing and climbing toward the heavens. It had been dark, as I was just walking around and singing, you know." The other nodded. Allie nodded, too, though she wasn't sure if she knew what the woman meant.

"There was so much light," she repeated, gesturing sharply with her right hand as though poking the darkness in front of her with a stick. She was silent for a long time. As she waited, Allie did not wonder if she would say more. She knew the women might not. Women as old as these had the old ways, and did not say as much aloud as younger ones did.

But she was content to sit, to listen to the insects, the turtle shell music of the dancers, their singing. She was comfortable there in the warm, welcoming dark, watching the flickers of the fires that ringed the dance ground cast into the night.

After a long silence, the old woman spoke again. "I think they have opened the earth. Earth Woman is being made to bring something forth. I think they do not know this, but my vision tells me it's so. Maybe they are preparing her for our new life. But many will try and stop the birth. We must watch, and wait. Maybe there will be some way to make sure her time comes as it should."

They said no more, after an hour or more Allie felt herself drifting off to sleep. She rose quietly and returned to her blanket, rolled herself up in it, and slept.

But when the dirty little justice of the peace said he would sign the papers saying she was old enough to enlist in the army, she remembered the woman's words. Something in her leaped with joy as he spoke; something said, "Go to the white man's war. You will learn what is needful there."

And so she went. And by another odd twist of circumstance, she was in New Mexico on leave the summer of 1945, had driven down to the southern mountains with some friends where they camped out in the mountains near Alamagordo. And there they witnessed the truth of the old woman's tale. "Oh, the light, the light," that old woman had said, and in her memory Allie saluted her, repeated, "so much light, oh, the light." Yes, that was why she had joined the army; so she could witness the birth of Sun Woman.

"An eagle am I." She needed the song often. She spent so much time with heterosexual women, so much energy protecting herself from discovery. The eagle had given her the song as a protection and a reminder that freedom was a lonely and bloodthirsty affair. It had come to her, sailing in the high sky over the peaks that towered above her small camp after several days during which she had been seeking and praying. She had been seeking an answer; praying for a sign—a vision, maybe; a dream; a talking stick—whatever the supernaturals might send her way in answer to her voice, calling them. And the song was not all of what they sent. No, they had been generous, that she knew; and also that their generosity would exact its own terrible price before the doing was done. Still, she had been grateful. Not softly so, of course; softness was another way. But what she had seen let her know her place in the dance of things, and made a circumstance that could be bitter had she gone in that direction with it, rather than a source of strong pride and determination. Vindication, maybe; certainly hot-blooded fierceness of joy. "An eagle am I," now she chanted, shouting. Letting go of the steering wheel momentarily. Reaching her arms over and behind her head. Stretching herself as the eagle had stretched herself, singing. Feeling the speed of flight as the car sped homeward in the gathering dark, arms stretching into the dusk behind her head. Then returning them to the wheel, she laughed. "And queer as hell."

After she had come down from the mountain, she had found a job in Seattle, settled into a life that was reasonably satisfactory. She worked at the university as a records clerk, though she had had some training as a technician in the army. The job was boring and tedious, and the salary wasn't much, but there were compensations. She believed that eventually the job would lead somewhere, given her special job in the army and her almost obsessive interest in postwar technology. She believed that Seattle was some kind of mystic center, both of the future and of the ancient earth of the tribal people. Her life there was free of the sense of oppression she had grown up with, and though she returned home as often as she could afford to, she returned to the Northwest like a magnetized needle to magnetic north. She felt a strange kinship to this place, its cool waters and pale sun, its seemingly endlesss rain. And there were other benefits. There was a community of lesbians, of sorts, that had grown up around their army days' bar, the Silver Slipper, a lesbian bar that was discreetly tucked away on the second floor of one of the downtown buildings.

She had been introduced to the bar by her first lover, a captain who was her C.O. Barbara—Bee they called her—had been military all the way. Correct and crisp, nearly brutal, she swaggered through her days and staggered through her nights. She was a heavy drinker, but then everyone was, and she held it well—at least until they got her back to her quarters, or until it was very late and her staggering and occasional bouts of terrifying rage would go unremarked by anyone with superior status or a desire to do her harm.

From the first time she saw Bee, shortly after arriving on base the spring of 1944, Allie had felt her stomach go weak with desire every time the woman had looked at her, her honey-colored hair, crisp and coldly shining under her cap. From the first time she saw her, Allie had wanted her. Bee was not the first woman Allie felt that erotic charge around, but Bee was the first who did much about it.

She called Allie to her quarters one night, late, and questioned her sharply about her work that day. Allie answered, feeling only mildly worried; she had faced frightening white authorities often in her life, so often that she was all but indifferent to their power. She knew it was only physical power in the end, and she was accustomed to beatings, solitary confinement, and social ostracism. Being deprived of white company was not much of a punishment, and branding her as socially unacceptable, deviant, unwanted, was the same as naming her Indian. And military prison might be rough, but so was her life. The way she saw it, the worst had already happened. There was little worse that they could threaten her with.

But Captain Brandon, after her interrogation, during which she had stared at Allie quite boldly, almost as though she was angry, abruptly, surprisingly, offered her some wine, invited her to stay and play a game of chess. Allie took the wine but refused the game, saying she didn't know how to play it. She wanted to stay but couldn't think how.

She needn't have worried. Bee thought of everything. She

seemed to understand how Allie felt about her, and after a time she sat near her on the couch where she had directed her to be seated when she offered her wine. She refilled Allie's glass, turning her body in such a way that Allie could see the line of her throat as it blended toward the curve of her breast beneath her stiffly starched shirt. Allie had been ready for many kinds of trouble, for any kind, she had thought in her tough, youthful innocence.

But desire, now. Wanting. Seeing Captain Brandon's hair soft in the low light of her quarters. Seeing her neck gleaming as soft as polished turquoise stones, river rocks, agate, quartz, in the small vee her slightly opened blouse revealed. And why didn't she wear her tie? Well, it was evening. She wasn't on duty. And something else: the captain's face seemed softer, her eyes gray, receiving, not flat and hard as they were during the day. Now all this was of interest to Allie. Of interest and growing excitement.

This made Allie smile in herself, coil her muscles in another kind of tension, toss her head however slightly as she responded to Brandon's questions about her life, whether she liked the service, the work she did. Made her answer with less cynicism than she would have in another place, to another face, made her begin to notice her breath catching as it came in or out of her throat. Made her bold enough to look the captain directly in the eye, drink her wine without moving her gaze, like she saw them doing in the movies. Maybe white women thought a good stare was a sex signal. She decided to try it, hoping it would work, somewhat surprised at her daring but under it feeling somehow that what she was feeling and thinking about her C.O. was what was expected of her in any case.

Not that she wasn't afraid. This was something to be afraid of. Suppose they did something, whatever it was that two women did? Something like what she and a couple of girls in boardingschool had done—kissing, playing with each other, shy and filled with laughter, bold and scared they'd be caught. She'd always wondered what they'd do if they found out, going so far sometimes as to imagine what she would say as one of the matrons was slapping her or locking her in the tiny closet they kept for uncooperative children, for those who thought they might defy a rule or who, not understanding enough English to obey a rule quickly, came under the punishing disapproval of their keepers.

Luckily, she had never found out. She'd had her share of run-ins with them, of course, but never over something so unthinkable as sex with a boy or a girl. She was pretty sure they'd come unglued entirely if they knew about the girls' sex games in the dark, and truly, even to scare herself, she didn't like to spend much time thinking about what they might do to her if they found out. Maybe they'd just starve her. To death. She'd heard of that happening to some boy, one she didn't know well but who suddenly disappeared from class and meals and never came back. She thought about her peril as she listened to the C.O. answering her queries in a quiet, Oklahoma drawl. She was sure that if this woman was putting the make on her, she'd be very, very happy to be made. And that also frightened her a little.

Suppose the woman there was only toying with her, testing her, trying to find her out? Suppose she wound up wanting the captain, the captain not wanting her? But then she'd look at the woman, at the pale skin lightly flushed, pearly, the strong square hands holding the wineglass, holding the bottle to pour more into their glasses. Allie put her thoughts behind her eyes, like putting her eyes behind dark glasses. She was barely eighteen, and while she had a lot of experience in war, and some experience in sex from hooking and cruising and hanging out, she didn't have any at all in loving women. She looked at her hands, wondered if they were weak.

She felt the burning in her crotch that knit it to her belly as though they were one organ, a limb or a heart, a head. And as she sat and answered to what was asked, and grew more and more tense, more and more languorous with her inward heat, dully pulsing with wine and desire, feeling her throat thickening, her voice deepening, hearing her breath wing its way past her nostrils, Captain Brandon leaned forward, took hold of Allie's wrist, looked for some time appraisingly into her eyes. Then nodded briskly, some question asked and answered in that moment. She stood, drawing Allie to her until their breasts touched, until their breasts fell into the softness of each other. Then slowly, deliberately, the captain kissed Allie, and that was all there was to it, and just like that, swiftly and silently as a deer pauses a moment then vanishes into the bush, Allie was taken by that twilight world, made a citizen of it, an outcast who forever would belong to wilderness, and there would be at home.

They had stories about it, the Indian people. Some of them, not her tribe, but her friends, had told her about Deer Woman, how she would come to a dance, so beautiful, so enchanting. She would choose you to dance with, circling the drum slowly, circling, circling in the light that blazed darkly from the tall fires that ringed the dance ground; she would dance with you, her elbow just touching yours, her shawl spread carefully around her shoulders and arms, held wih breathtaking perfect precision over her cocked right arm, torso making just the right sideward bow, tiny steps perfect in their knowing of the drum. She would dance you, dance into you, holding your gaze with her eyes, for if your eyes looked down at her feet you would see her hooves and the spell would be broken. And after a time she would incline her head, say, perhaps, come, and you would follow. Away from the fire and the dancing, into the brush, into the night. And you would not return, or if you did, it would be as somebody else.

The woman undressed Allie slowly, shifting her gaze from Allie's breasts, belly, the dark thin brush of hair beneath it, to her eyes. She held Allie frozen with them, looking at her intently, as though commanding her to remain still for this deliberate unclothing. She knelt to draw Allie's panties down her legs, gesturing for her to lift her feet, one, then the other, and when the panties were free, Bee tossed them aside and stood, a foot or so away, and looked Allie up and down as though she were reporting for roll call before dawn.

But her lips were slightly parted, her skin was slightly moist. Allie could hear her breathing, see her chest rise and fall beneath her stiffly starched blouse. And after Bee had looked her fill, she gestured to the couch, took Allie again by the wrist, pulling down on it until Allie was sitting, half reclining on the couch. And she tugged at her arm again, and Allie allowed herself to be drawn down. She lay back and sighed deeply. Yes, she thought fiercely on fire, oh, yes, as she felt Bee's hands stroking her, pinching her nipples tightly erect, felt her hands stroking her head, her face, her breasts, felt Barbara's lips cool and demanding on her cheek, in the hollow of her throat. "Yes, yes," she whispered, "give it to me, oh, please." Rocking her body softly, turning her head from side to side, a low moan beginning somewhere in her diaphragm, and felt the woman parting her legs with cool hands, felt something wet and cool on her burning cunt, and raising her head slightly, looking down, saw those gray eyes watching her sharply, felt Bee's tongue push into her, and fell back then against the rough scratching of the couch, dizzy with fire, exultant with joy.

After that night she was one of the captain's girls. There were several of them, young women mostly, who answered to Barbara Brandon's beck and call and were happy to do so. In turn, she often took them off base to eat, to shop, and on weekends to dance and drink themselves senseless at the Silver Slipper.

Allie never wondered about the arrangement. She accepted it, just as she accepted Bee's refusal to let Allie make love to her. She seldom understood what went on in white people's heads, and never expected herself to. Sometimes the others would gossip, and she would listen. That was part of her life, she thought, to listen and learn. Watch and wait, that was what the old woman had said, and so she did. They talked about how the captain protected them from discovery for being gay girls, how she had such a special position in the service because she worked on the development and staffing of the computer, because she kept her private life private and only took lovers she could trust. In a way she was like a godmother to them, and most of them had a real crush on her. She was mentor, protector, and commander, and they giggled and gossiped endlessly about how women in uniforms turned them on.

Some of them expected to get married after the war, but while they were in uniform they saw no harm in playing around, as they put it. In fact, they preferred being part of what they named "The Queen Bee's Hive" rather than dating the dreary procession of officers and enlisted men who tried to make it with them. As Ruby, a muscular blonde with untamable hair and a mouth to match, phrased it, "At least spit ain't potent."

When the war ended, Allie considered reenlisting. She didn't want to lose her circle of friends, the first she'd known since leaving Oklahoma, and she didn't want to lose the noticeably more comfortable life she had enjoyed for over a year. The idea of going back to no hope at home, or to drifting through the civilian white world, filled her with fear. She didn't know what she would do, out there, without a uniform, a ready-made social group, an income. And there was her dream, her knowledge—whatever you called it. She knew she was in this world for some particular work, that she had a clear road to walk, though she didn't have much of an idea of what it might be. But she suspected it had something to do with being a lesbian and with the new technology that was being developed here, in the army. And she was sure that on the outside she would have no chance of being even remotely associated with any of it.

If she was lucky, she figured she could be a waitress, maybe find work in an office as a file clerk, maybe in a hospital or nursing home emptying bed pans and scrubbing floors. The prospects didn't seem attractive. She could return to prostitution, but after the past year she felt slightly sick when she thought of it. It wasn't because she had developed a case of Christian morality, but because she had developed her previously unrealized but always present under the surface, lurking there like brightly colored fish lurk in the shadowy cool of a deep lake, unseen, but there, love for women, for a woman, for herself as a woman, as a sweet, warm pulsing cunt, longing, reaching, tasting nipples, glossy hair and skin, eyes that could watch the intense face of a woman fingering her deep inside, a woman's buried face between her thighs. That knowing, surging glee, desire, joy, and life-affirming power that burst into flame within when Bee came in the room, when Ruby drawled another obscene observation, when Darlene giggled gleefully and lowered her short-lashed lids when she'd drawn a winning hand at poker, was what she did not intend to give up, to ever go without again.

But one night Bee called her in and, after making love to her, told Allie her tour was about up and that she was getting out. She said Allie should get out of the service. "You don't belong here, you know, and I'm retiring so I won't be here to run interference for you anymore." She had sighed and after a long pause said, "You know, our period of grace is over, Honey Bun." Allie grinned at the name. The girls called the captain Queen Bee because she called them Honey Bun.

Bee's voice roughened uncharacteristically. It sounded harshly over her next words, conveying a feeling of metal scraping against unoiled metal as she spoke. "This is no joking matter, Alice," she said, raising her voice slightly. "There's gonna be hell to pay around here soon. They'll be going after the lezzies, and unless you want to stay and stool for them so you can keep your playpen rights or get busted all the way down to minus nothing, you'd better get out. I can stay, of course. I don't think they'd go after me because of my rank, because letting a queer get this far wouldn't look so good for them, but I'm getting out. I'm nearly fifty, and I have retirement coming, and the G.I. bill, and plans for the rest of my life." She smiled. "I have a little house all picked out here, and I'm gonna stay. But I'm warning you, for your own good, get out while the getting's good."

Allie had been stunned by all of this that night, but over the next few weeks she thought about what Bee had said, and what she had not said, and decided to take the older woman's advice and walk while she could. Honorable discharge could be something that worked in her favor, maybe. With a dishonorable, she didn't have a chance.

They all went to the Slipper for a last celebration and danced and wept and promised to keep in touch. The next day Allie ironed her uniforms for the last time, packed them in mothballs, put on her civvies, and went out of the barracks to see what life had for her that day. After she got a room to live in and stashed her stuff, she decided to head for the hills, to just get back into place in the universe, and it was on that trip she had gotten the eagle's gift and had learned a bit more about how her life would go.

During the next few years Allie drifted away from most of the old gang who'd stayed in Seattle, still seeing Bee occasionally, though. While in the service, they had worked with the first computers, Mark I and then, for a few months before they left the army, EN-

IAC—more formally, the vacuum-tube monster called an Electronic Numerical Integrator And Calculator. Under Bee's direction, Allie and several of the others of Bee's crew had worked as operators of ENIAC's manually operated switchboard. This job in the service was a connection they shared over the years, as Bee got an executive's position at Lockheed, where she oversaw the installation and operation of their first computer, while Allie had eventually secured a job as a clerk typist at the small University of Washington that led to her position in their computer system soon after they instituted it in the middle 1950s.

It was toward the end of that job, about fifteen years after leaving the army, that Allie went to a sing at a nearby reservation and where she met Eddie Raven.

She had been there for a couple of hours already, listening to the speakers, watching the dancers as they were presented to receive their formal acknowledgment as dancers for the people, when the door opened and through the smoke of the fire she could see the tall, slender figure of a young man, another of those being honored, she had thought. He was dressed in western clothes, boots, pants, shirt, and Stetson, all black. The hat was adorned with a silver and turquoise concho belt and a feather that rode its neatly shaped brim. He stood for a moment, framed in the driving rain that swept through the blanket he had raised to enter the longhouse. His presence was commanding in some indefinable way, as though he was the son of a very important man, or as though he had already won many contests, told many tales, sung many songs. Then, as the figure stepped into the smoky room, Allie saw that the young man was a woman of maybe twenty years, a woman whose deep eyes were quiet and still with a certain poise and power that Allie had never seen before. The woman sitting on the bench next to her whispered with a sibilant intake of breath, "Eddie Raven."

"What?" Allie had said. Bemused. Mesmerized. Electrified. She was having trouble with her hearing.

The woman inclined her head closer to Allie's. "That girl that just came in, over there." She gestured in Raven's direction, using chin and lips expertly. "Her name is Eddie Raven."

After the formalities, while the women were serving supper, stew from the huge iron pots, platters of fish, piles of rainbow bread, Allie found herself watching the girl. "I must be getting neurotic," she thought. She felt bereft every time Eddie Raven disappeared from view, every time she was engaged in conversation with someone. Allie watched her every move, holding her breath and looking away every time Raven's eye seemed about to catch hers.

When the men and guests had been served, the women who were hosting the feed filled their plates and made their way through the crowded longhouse to find places to sit where they could enjoy a good gossip and a good view of the goings-on. Even though she had helped the family get the food served, and so was part of that group, Allie couldn't bring herself to join the clusters of women, and instead found a place in the shadows of a far corner where she lowered herself to the floor. She ate, not tasting the food though usually it was a source of great comfort to her, connecting her somehow to home. Though, of course, these were far different people from her own, and their food was very different from that served at green corn dances or other community gatherings back in Oklahoma, still there was something very similar between them, maybe in the feeling of the food though not its taste, maybe in the sense she had while eating it of being settled and accepted in the boundless mothering of the earth from which these foods came. Thinking this, she glanced at the piece of bread in her hand, mutely pale, limply white. Well, almost all of them, she thought wryly, squeezing the slice into a tiny, moist ball and dropping it on her plate. She shrugged, aware that even though the stuff was awful, it was also some kind of connector to home, and usually she ate it with a mild sense of amusement and enjoyment.

"That stuff is only good with cheap strawberry jam on it," a voice near her said.

Startled, Allie looked to her left. She was suddenly not breathing too well. Raven was hunkering down near her, grinning, her black eyes gleaming like ripe blackberries in the morning sun.

She grinned spontaneously, her mood suddenly swinging to mindless joy. "Or with tons of lard and some sugar!"

The younger woman looked puzzled. "That's how we used to eat it at boardingschool, sometimes. It was our special treat," Allie explained.

Raven nodded, comprehending. She edged slightly closer to Allie. "I've been watching you," she said, looking down modestly. There was a slight, quizzical smile on her thin, wide lips. She had the straightest teeth Allie had ever seen. Allie pretended nonchalance and put a large morsel of salmon in her mouth. "Sweet, sweet fish," she thought. She felt her face get warm.

She hoped Raven hadn't heard her, then caught herself. "Of course she didn't, you goose," she thought. "You didn't say it out loud." But she was aware that Raven had shot her an amused glance when she thought it. She choked. "I noticed you when you came in. I've never seen you before," she managed to say over the constriction of her throat. She swallowed the fish, then sipped some broth from the bowl of stew.

"You shouldn't have thrown that bread," Raven said. "It's good for chasing fish bone." She rose. "I'll get you a piece."

Allie shook her head, now unable to speak. Her eyes were watering. "I think I'm gonna die right here," she thought. "How romantic. How undignified." She waved her hand at Raven, managed to gasp, "No, no. I'm all right." She coughed spasmodically.

"Raise your hands over your head," Raven said. Too overcome with coughing to argue, Allie did as she was told. The coughing subsided. She drew a slow breath, then another.

"I've been away for a while," Raven said. Her eyes flickered, maybe with the flickering glow of the fire. "I haven't seen you here before, either."

"I don't come as regularly as I'd like," Allie said. "The folks are good to have me, and I'm so far from home here, it's lucky they're here."

"Where you from?"

"Oklahoma. I'm Cheyenne."

"I'm Mississippesh."

"What's that?" Allie had never heard of Mississippesh, but there were hundreds of tribes—she couldn't know all, or even most of them.

"We're extinct." Raven gave a short laugh.

Allie grinned. "Well, so's everyone."

"Except the Cherokee and the Sioux," Raven agreed. Then, with a sly glance at Allie, "And the brave Cheyenne."

"Don't forget the Navajo and the Iroquois, the secret weapon of the government in the war." She spoke without inflection.

"No," Raven agreed calmly. "Or the drunk drowned heroic Pima, good old Ira Hayes, winner of a Congressional Medal of Honor and raiser of the American flag on Iwo Jima, conqueror of the Pacific theater, and all that. I know my history, at least my seventh-grade civics." There was a slightly bitter bite to her otherwise gentle voice.

Allie was stopped for a moment. She remembered how young this tall, curiously disturbing, profoundly self-possessed girl must be. "Civics?" she asked. "What's civics? I think that was way after my time!"

"Some class they give in public schools nowadays—it's between history and geography. Current events, I guess they call it in some places. I bet they didn't teach it in the olden days," she joked.

Again Allie had the eerie feeling that Eddie Raven could read minds. "So where do the Mississippesh live? Or did live, I should say."

"We are one of the Algonquian peoples, one of the Anishenaabeg, or original human beings. Mr. Brewer, that's my grandfather, sort of, said we were originally from the stars, but then we got on turtle's back. Our stock got here through a little hanky-panky with Earth Woman or First Mother, Auch'se^{ch}. Then we lived around the Great Lakes. Then we moved south and west from those grounds when the whites started moving in from the east. I'm the last of us," she said matter-of-factly, "and I live wherever I am."

After a reflective silence Allie said, "I came here during the war—the Second World War, that is," grinning lightly. "It had a special quality to it, or so it seemed to me. Maybe I just like the rain. And I could get decent work, and some of my friends from the service were settling here, so anyway, here I am."

"I came out here when I was fourteen, to live with my aunt, my mother's uncle's wife. She adopted me after my folks died. But they live on another reserve, northwest of here. Anyway, I've been around this area for most of seven years, but I've been traveling a lot for the past two or three—that, and going to school."

"Do you come here often?"

"Some. I haven't been to one of these doings for a couple of years, but I come by to visit Betty and Raymond and their family from time to time. We're sort of related."

At one end of the longhouse the band, which consisted of two elderly fiddlers and a young, handsome boy proudly bent over a gleaming guitar, was tuning up. People were moving around, putting away food and dishes. Allie looked around, and noticed that most of the family was occupied with clean-up. She stood. "Guess it's k.p. time," she said. Raven uncoiled her long limbs and stood. Her high-heel boots gleamed modestly beneath the sharply creased edge of her black, fitted western pants. She put out her hand, saying "I'm Eddie Raven."

Allie took it, pressing it softly for a moment, then letting go. "I know," she said. "That means something special, I think." She shook her head sharply as though to clear it. "I'm Allie Hawker." She grinned.

"Raven and Hawker." The black-shirted young woman drawled. "We should be an Indian comic team."

"Yeah." Allie nodded, thinking "Well, one of us is pretty funny. Let's hope the other one is, too." They carried dishes to the house where several women were chattering and laughing as they tidied up after the feast.

After cleaning up, Raven sauntered over to Allie. "Did you know your name means lost or lost one in their language?" indicating the two or three women of the house with a slight gesture of her head.

"Yeah, it's been one of our favorite jokes around here for some time," Allie said. "That and a thousand variations on it. You know."

"Like, if you're lost, I bet I can find you?" Raven eyed Allie levelly.

"Shoot," Allie said, gazing coolly back at the vibrant, handsome face, thinking "Okay, little tease, let's see if you mean it." She had to make an effort to hold her gaze steady as Raven's. "I'm about as lost as any little black sheep."

"Finders keepers, then," Raven said in a soft, startlingly husky voice, and grabbing Allie's hand, she pulled her out into the everlasting rain.

MAURICE KENNY
MOHAWK

WINKTE*

He told me that if nature puts a burden on a man by making him different, it also gives him a power.
—John (Fire) Lame Deer, Sioux Medicine Man

We are special to the Sioux!
They gave us respect for strange powers
Of looking into the sun, the night.
They paid us with horses not derision.

To the Cheyenne we were no curiosity!
We were friends or wives of brave warriors
Who hunted for our cooking pots
Who protected our tipis from Pawnee.

We went to the mountain for our puberty vision.
No horse or lance or thunderbird
Crossed the dreaming eye which would have sent us
Into war or the hunter's lonely woods.
To some song floated on mountain air.
To others colors and design appeared on clouds.
To a few words fell from the eagle's wing,
And they took to the medicine tent,
And in their holiness made power
For the people of the Cheyenne Nation.
There was space for us in the village.

**Sioux word for male homosexual.*
Previously published in Gay Sunshine *and* Manroot.

The Crow and Ponca offered deerskin
When the decision to avoid the warpath was made,
And we were accepted into the fur robes
Of a young warrior, and lay by his flesh
And knew his mouth and warm groin.
Or we married (a second wife) to the chief.
And if we fulfilled our duties, he smiled
And gave us his grandchildren to care for.

We were special to the Sioux, Cheyenne, Ponca
And the Crow who valued our worth and did not spit
Names at our lifted skirts nor kicked our nakedness.
We had power with the people!

And if we cared to carry the lance, or dance
Over enemy scalps and take buffalo
Then that, too, was good for the Nation,
And contrary to our stand we walked backwards.

MAURICE KENNY
MOHAWK

PIMA

Eyes of desert night
word/tongue peaches of Arizona
orchards planted by old women
praising as I praise your mouth,
eyes behind shadows.

Pima, your beauty touched
I quiver, store words in a basket
as women store fruit,
and your smiles of autumn
on a bar stool in Brooklyn.

You flee via Pan-American
to blooming cactus, silence.
Desert afternoon will fire
your flesh; mine
cools with morning.

Previously published in River Styx *(1984).*

MAURICE KENNY
MOHAWK

UNITED

For Randy

Moon music moved them together
across nights of bat-darkness,
earth drummed by naked feet
that beats Nevada mountains,
high hills of Mohawk country.

Though old Medicine Men,
prodded by priest and politician,
no longer wear robes;
nor boys, geld and tender,
gather holy corn
nor are celebrated on the warpath
and taken in love by strong warriors . . .
they remain in lodges and languages
where the vision is honored,
and grandfathers know Nations will gather.

Moon music moved them together;
breechclouts left at the door,
straight firs . . . ponderosa to cedar . . .
naked, crossed in the star-burst of dawn:
bent, spent, broken in deep valleys.
The first frenzied dance finished.
Wovoka shook hands with Cornplanter.
Earth parts for the seed of their firs.

Previously published in Gay Sunshine *26/27 (Winter 1975/76) and* Only as Far as Brooklyn *(Boston: Good Gay Poets, 1980).*

DANIEL-HARRY STEWARD

WINTU

COYOTE AND TEHOMA

Clever Coyote
Could change his identity and become
A cricket, a mouse, or the wind.
Coyote could always find a woman and
Cunningly make her submit.
But there are stories of how Coyote
Pursued Tehoma, God of the smoking mountain.
Tehoma was powerful
Tehoma was strengthful
Tehoma was well made
Tehoma was radiant of limb.
Walking the hillsides
Or running Mill Creek
He awed the lesser spirits
With his prowess and skill
And they made him guardian
Of the smoking mountain.
He listened as crow described
The extent of the underworld.
He built the chambers and flues
As hawk and wren advised.
Carefully he carved the furnaces
As muskrat and squirrel directed.
As Tehoma became more wise in judgment
And handsome of form the lesser spirits
Proclaimed him their Chief and God
Of the smoking mountain.
As the years went by word spread up and down

Eagle Kachina Dancers, 18x24, tempera on bristol, 1982.
Joe Lawrence Lembo.

The valley about the God of the smoking mountain,
How the spirits revered his image
And waited upon his word,
How he had changed the sacred mountain
And stoked the fires until sometimes at night
A glow from the depths would fill the
Sky with dancing lights.
Coyote heard these tales and became curious.
Who is this man-God?
Deer has told me of his invincible manner.
Eagle has seen him cut off his hair
With a black glass blade.
Cougar paces him as he runs,
And mouse, watching him naked by the light of the
Fiery furnace, says indeed his body is finely
Honed muscle and glistens like shining gold.
Wonder captured Coyote and made him imagine
What this God would be like
To see and smell and touch.
Coyote fell from curiosity to enchantment.
Boiling a tea from klark-ia and red bud
He sank into a deep dream sleep
And when he woke he was tall, regal, and handsome.
Packing some fine goods he walked up Deer Creek
And when he reached the smoking mountain
He called upon the spirits of the wind and earth
To follow him as he descended into the
Labyrinth between the sky and the center of the world.
The path was hot and winding so Coyote
Took off his skins and walked naked into the depths.
Deep inside the mountain he came unseen upon
Tehoma and watched as he loaded the furnaces,
Supple limbs straining,
Every sinew taut and rippling.
This man is mine, said Coyote to himself.
He will bask in my admiration and
Be part of my spirit.
Coyote moved forward and as they stood

Face to face the Gods were each one of a kind,
Each a handsome man
Each a well-made man.
Tehoma greeted his guest
And brought dried meat and seeds.
I am Tehoma, keeper of this smoking mountain.
This is my dominion, a gift from the spirits
Who are all around.
Coyote offered shelled acorns brought from the valley
And as he placed them in the hands of Tehoma
He breathed deeply of the smell of this man
And looked upon his youthful body.
I am Coyote he said and we are both Gods,
And grizzly, salmon, eagle and all shape
Of spirits are with me.
Let us eat and celebrate said Coyote
Of our meeting in this sacred mountain.
But first let us have games and wrestle
As I think we are evenly matched.
Your room is wide and the fires are blazing.
Tehoma smiled with confidence.
He could beat Coyote.
They marked off the wrestling ground,
Pacing the boundary and then began their game.
Sweat ran from their bodies as they caught,
Turned, lunged, and held,
Eye to eye pressing flesh into flesh.
The mountain shook and smoked,
Trembling as they wrestled from gods to lovers.
Such was the meeting, such was their passion
That the spirits, amused, moved outside the mountain.
Coyote lay naked next to Tehoma
Their bodies entwined in sleep so deep
They did not see the furnaces blazing,
Flaming, blocking the smoking chimney.
Before the two could wake and rise
The furnaces blew out and sent the mountain
Exploding into the air with burning fire

All the rock
All the snows
All the trees
All the unlucky spirits.
In the thunder and the dark
Coyote woke and searched for Tehoma
But his lover could not be found.
In the din and blackness
Coyote gathered those living spirits
He could find and went across the valley
To Yolla Bolly mountain and waited
Many days for the sun to appear.
Eagle returned saying the land was white
And deep with powder for leagues in all directions.
Grizzly said the rivers were choked with
Fallen trees and dead spirits.
Coyote spoke to the wind for wings
And they flew over the smoking mountain.
Dismayed, he found the mountain had disappeared
Replaced with a gaping crater filled
With a thousand smokes.
But Tehoma was nowhere to be found.
Crow called all the spirits together
And they brought comfort to Coyote.
Look yonder
Said owl pointing to the evening sky.
Tehoma is there in the stars.
See him there with those spirits who loved him.
You are a God who became a man,
Said crow to Coyote,
And Tehoma was a man who became a God.
He could not have done as you have done
So his spirit has been changed into the stars,
Glowing in the night.
And now he and the other spirits
Look down and wait for a time to return.
We will honor them said Coyote
We will sign to them that they will come back.

Let us build a mound that can be seen for many miles
So that Tehoma will know where to find us,
Even from south valley
Even from Shasta
Even from Yolla Bolly.
And so they built the mound like a beacon
On the north side of the fuming crater,
Built it high and round to catch the summer sun
And winter snows.
And still today the gentle spirits live
In the place called Tehoma,
And at edge of twilight you can hear Coyote
Calling to his lover who waits above
In the starry starry night.

BETH BRANT

BAY OF QUINTE MOHAWK

COYOTE LEARNS A NEW TRICK

Coyote thought of a good joke.

She laughed so hard, she almost wanted to keep it to herself. But what good is a joke if you can't trick creatures into believing one thing is true when Coyote knows truth is only what she makes it?

She laughed and snorted and got out her sewing machine and made herself a wonderful outfit. Brown tweed pants with a zipper in the front and very pegged bottoms. A white shirt with pointed collar and french cuffs. A tie from a scrap of brown and black striped silk she had found in her night rummagings. She had some brown cowboy boots in her closet and spit on them, polishing them with her tail. She found some pretty stones that she fashioned into cufflinks for her dress shirt.

She bound her breasts with an old diaper left over from her last litter, and placed over this a sleeveless undershirt that someone had thrown in the garbage dump. It had a few holes and smelled strong, but that went with the trick. She buttoned the white shirt over the holes and smell, and wound the tie around her neck, where she knotted it with flair.

She stuffed more diapers into her underpants so it looked like she had a swell inside. A big swell.

She was almost ready, but needed something to hide her brown hair. Then she remembered a fedora that had been abandoned by an old friend, and set it at an angle over one brown eye.

She looked in the mirror and almost died laughing. She looked like a very dapper male of style.

Reprinted with the permission of Firebrand Books from Mohawk Trail *(Ithaca, NY: Firebrand Books, 1985).*

Out of her bag of tricks, she pulled a long silver chain and looped it from her belt to her pocket, where it swayed so fine.

Stepping outside her lair, she told her pups she'd be back after she had performed this latest bit of magic. They waved her away with "Oh, Mom, what is it this time?"

Subduing her laughter, she walked slowly, wanting each creature to see her movements and behold the wondrous Coyote strutting along.

A hawk spied her, stopped in mid-circle, then flew down to get a good look. "My god, I've never seen anything like it!" And Hawk screamed and carried on, her wing beating her leg as she slapped it with each whoop of laughter. Then she flew back into the sky in hot pursuit of a juicy rat she had seen earlier.

Coyote was undaunted. She knew she looked good, and besides, hawks have been known to have no sense of humor.

Dancing along, Coyote saw Turtle, as usual, caught between the road and the marsh. Stepping more quickly, Coyote approached Turtle and asked, in a sarcastic manner, if Turtle needed directions. Turtle fixed her with an astonished eye and hurriedly moved toward the weeds, grumbling about creatures who were too weird to *even* bother with.

Coyote's plan was not going so well.

Then she thought of Fox. That la-di-da female who was forever grooming her pelt and telling stories about how clever and sly she was. "She's the one!" said Coyote.

So she sauntered up to Fox's place, whistling and perfecting her new deep voice and showful walk. Knocking on Fox's door, she brushed lint and hairs from her shirt and crushed the hat more securely on her head. Fox opened the door, and her eyes got very large with surprise and admiration.

"Can I help you?" she said with a brush of her eyelashes.

Coyote said, "I seem to be lost. Can you tell a man like me where to find a dinner to refresh myself after my long walk?"

Fox said, "Come on in. I was just this minute fixing a little supper and getting ready to have something cool to drink. Won't you join me? It wouldn't do for a stranger to pass through my place and not feel welcomed."

Coyote was impressed. This was going better than she had planned. She stiffled a laugh.

"Did you say something?" Fox seemed eager to know.

"I was just admiring your red fur. Mighty pretty."

"Oh, it's nothing. Inherited, you know. But I really stand in admiration of your hat and silver chain. Where did you ever find such things?"

"Well, I'm a traveling man myself. Pick up things here and there. Travel mostly at night. You can find a lot of things at night. It sure smells good in here. You must be a fine cook."

Fox laughed. "I've been known to cook up a few things. Food is one of the more sensual pleasures in life, don't you think?" she said, pouring Coyote a glass of red wine. "But I can think of several things that are equally as pleasurable, can't you?" And she winked her red eye. Coyote almost choked on her wine. She realized that she had to get this joke back into her own paws.

"Say, you're a pretty female. Got a man around the house?"

Fox laughed and laughed and laughed, her red fur shaking. "No, there are no men around here. Just me and sometimes a few girlfriends that stay over." And Fox laughed and laughed and laughed, her long nose sniffing and snorting.

Coyote couldn't figure out why Fox laughed so much. Maybe she was nervous with such a fine-looking Coyote in her house. Why, I bet she's never seen the likes of me! But it's time to get on with the trick.

Now, Coyote's trick was to make a fool out of Fox. To get her all worked up, thinking Coyote was a male, then reveal her true female Coyote self. It would make a good story. How Fox thought she was so sly and smart, but a Coyote got the best of her. Why, Coyote could tell this story for years to come!

One thing led to another, as they often do. They ate dinner, drank a little more red wine. Fox batted her eyelashes so much, Coyote thought they'd fall off! But Coyote was having a good time, too. Now was the time.

"Hey, Fox, you seem like a friendly type. How about a roll in the hay?"

"I thought you'd never ask," said Fox, laughing and laughing.

Lying on Fox's pallet, having her body next to hers, Coyote thought maybe she'd wait a bit before playing the trick. Besides, it was fun to be rolling around with a red-haired female. And man oh man, she really could kiss. That tongue of hers sure knows a trick or two. And boy oh boy, that sure feels good, her paw on my back, rubbing and petting. And wow, I never knew foxes could do such things, moving her legs like that, pulling me down on top of her like that. And she makes such pretty noises, moaning like that. And her paw feels real good, unzipping my pants. And oh oh, she's going to find out the trick, and then what'll I do?

"Coyote! Why don't you take that ridiculous stuffing out of your pants. And take off that undershirt, it smells to high heaven. And let me untie that binder so we can get down to *serious* business."

Coyote had not fooled Fox. But somehow, playing the trick didn't seem so important anyway.

So Coyote took off her clothes, lay on top of Fox, her leg moving between Fox's open limbs. She panted and moved and panted some more and told herself that foxes were clever after all. In fact, they were downright smart with all the stuff they knew.

Mmmmm yeah, this Fox is pretty clever with all that stuff she knows. This is the best trick I ever heard of. Why didn't I think of it?

BETH BRANT
BAY OF QUINTE MOHAWK

A LONG STORY

Dedicated to my great-grandmothers,
Eliza Powless and Catherine Brant

About 40 Indian children took the train at this depot for the Philadelphia Indian School last Friday. They were accompanied by the government agent, and seemed a bright looking lot.
—The Northern Observer
(Massena, New York, July 20, 1892)

I am only beginning to understand what it means for a mother to lose a child.
—*Anna Demeter,* Legal Kidnapping
(Beacon Press, Boston, 1977)

1890

It has been two days since they came and took the children away. My body is greatly chilled. All our blankets have been used to bring me warmth. The women keep the fire blazing. The men sit. They talk among themselves. We are frightened by this sudden child-stealing. We signed papers, the agent said. This gave them rights to take our babies. It is good for them, the agent said. It will make them civilized, the agent said. I do not know *civilized.*

I hold myself tight in fear of flying apart in the air. The others try to feed me. Can they feed a dead woman? I have stopped talk-

Reprinted by permission of Firebrand Books from Mohawk Trail *(Ithaca, NY: Firebrand Books, 1985).*

Mattie Looks Homeward.
Hulleah Tsinhnahjinnie.

ing. When my mouth opens, only air escapes. I have used up my sound screaming their names—She Sees Deer! He Catches The Leaves! My eyes stare at the room, the walls of scrubbed wood, the floor of dirt. I know there are people here, but I cannot see them. I see a darkness, like the lake at New Moon. Black, unmoving. In the center, a picture of my son and daughter being lifted onto the train. My daughter wearing the dark blue, heavy dress. All of the girls dressed alike. Never have I seen such eyes! They burn into my head even now. My son. His hair cut. Dressed as the white men, his arms and legs covered by cloth that made him sweat. His face, streaked with tears. So many children crying, screaming. The sun on our bodies, our heads. The train screeching like a crow, sounding like laughter. Smoke and dirt pumping out of the insides of the train. So many people. So many children. The women, standing as if in prayer, our hands lifted, reaching. The dust sifting down on our palms. Our palms making motions at the sky. Our fingers closing like the claws of the bear.

I see this now. The hair of my son held in my hands. I rub the strands, the heavy braids coming alive as the fire flares and casts a bright light on the black hair. They slip from my fingers and lie coiled on the ground. I see this. My husband picks up the braids, wraps them in cloth; he takes the pieces of our son away. He walks outside, the eyes of the people on him. I see this. He will find a bottle and drink with the men. Some of the women will join him. They will end the night by singing or crying. It is all the same. I see this. No sounds of children playing games and laughing. Even the dogs have ceased their noise. They lay outside each doorway, waiting. I hear this. The voices of children. They cry. They pray. They call me. *Nisten ha.** I hear this. *Nisten ha.*

1978

I am wakened by the dream. In the dream my daughter is dead. Her father is returning her body to me in pieces. He keeps her heart. I thought I screamed . . . *Patricia!* I sit up in bed, swallowing air as if for nourishment. The dream remains in the air. I rise to go to her room. Ellen tries to lead me back to bed, but I have to see once again. I open her door. She is gone. The room empty, lonely. They said it was in her best interests. How can that be? She is only six, a baby who needs her mothers. She loves us. This has not happened. I will not believe this. Oh, god, I think I have died.

Night after night, Ellen holds me as I shake. Our sobs stifling the air in our room. We lie in our bed and try to give comfort. My mind can't think beyond last week when she left. I would have

**Mother.*

killed him if I'd had the chance! He took her hand and pulled her to the car. The look in his eyes of triumph. It was a contest to him, Patricia the prize. He will teach her to hate us. He will! I see her dear face. That face looking out the back window of his car. Her mouth forming the words *Mommy, Mama*. Her dark braids tied with red yarn. Her front teeth missing. Her overalls with the yellow flower on the pocket, embroidered by Ellen's hands. So lovingly she sewed the yellow wool. Patricia waiting quietly until she was finished. Ellen promising to teach her designs—chain stitch, french knot, split stitch. How Patricia told everyone that Ellen made the flower just for her. So proud of her overalls.

I open the closet door. Almost everything is gone. A few things hang there limp, abandoned. I pull a blue dress from the hanger and take it back to my room. Ellen tries to take it from me, but I hold on, the soft blue cotton smelling of my daughter. How is it possible to feel such pain and live? "Ellen?!" She croons my name. "Mary, Mary, I love you." She sings me to sleep.

1890

The agent was here to deliver a letter. I screamed at him and sent curses his way. I threw dirt in his face as he mounted his horse. He thinks I'm a crazy woman and warns me, "You better settle down, Annie." What can they do to me? I am a crazy woman. This letter hurts my hand. It is written in their hateful language. It is evil, but there is a message for me.

I start the walk up the road to my brother. He works for the whites and understands their meanings. I think about my brother as I pull the shawl closer to my body. It is cold now. Soon there will be snow. The corn has been dried and hangs from our cabin, waiting to be used. The corn never changes. My brother is changed. He says that *I* have changed and bring shame to our clan. He says I should accept the fate. But I do not believe in the fate of child-stealing. There is evil here. There is much wrong in our village. My brother says I am a crazy woman because I howl at the sky every evening. He is a fool. I am calling the children. He says the people are becoming afraid of me because I talk to the air and laugh like the raven overhead. But I am talking to the children. They need to hear the sound of me. I laugh to cheer them. They cry for us.

This letter burns my hands. I hurry to my brother. He has taken the sign of the wolf from over the doorway. He pretends to be like those who hate us. He gets more and more like the child-stealers. His eyes move away from mine. He takes the letter from me and begins the reading of it. I am confused. This letter is from two strangers with the names Martha and Daniel. They say they are learning civilized ways. Daniel works in the fields, growing food for the school. Martha cooks and is being taught to sew aprons. She will be going to live with the schoolmaster's wife. She will be a live-in girl. What is a *live-in girl?* I shake my head. The words sound the same to me. I am afraid of Martha and Daniel, these strangers who know my name. My hands and arms are becoming numb.

I tear the letter from my brother's fingers. He stares at me, his eyes traitors in his face. He calls after me, "Annie! Annie!" That is not my name! I run to the road. That is not my name! There is no Martha! There is no Daniel! This is witch work. The paper burns and burns. At my cabin, I quickly dig a hole in the field. The earth is hard and cold, but I dig with my nails. I dig, my hands feeling weaker. I tear the paper and bury the scraps. As the earth drifts and settles, the names Martha and Daniel are covered. I look to the sky and find nothing but endless blue. My eyes are blinded by the color. I begin the howling.

1978

When I get home from work, there is a letter from Patricia. I make coffee and wait for Ellen, pacing the rooms of our apartment. My back is sore from the line, bending over and down, screwing the handles on the doors of the flashy cars moving by. My work protects me from questions, the guys making jokes at my expense. But some of them touch my shoulder lightly and briefly as a sign of understanding. The few women, eyes averted or smiling in sympathy. No one talks. There is no time to talk. No room to talk, the noise taking up all space and breath.

I carry the letter with me as I move from room to room. Finally I sit at the kitchen table, turning the paper around in my hands. Patricia's printing is large and uneven. The stamp has been glued on halfheartedly and is coming loose. Each time a letter arrives, I dread it, even as I long to hear from my child. I hear Ellen's key in the door. She walks into the kitchen, bringing the smell of the hospital with her. She comes toward me, her face set in new lines, her uniform crumpled and stained, her brown hair pulled back in an imitation of a french twist. She knows there is a letter. I kiss her and bring mugs of coffee to the table. We look at each other. She reaches for my hand, bringing it to her lips. Her hazel eyes are steady in her round face.

I open the letter. *Dear Mommy. I am fine. Daddy got me a new bike. My big teeth are coming in. We are going to see Grandma for my birthday. Daddy got me new shoes. Love, Patricia.* She doesn't ask about Ellen. I imagine her father standing over her, coaxing her, coaching her. The letter becomes ugly. I tear it in bits and scatter them out the window. The wind scoops the pieces into a tight fist before strewing them in the street. A car drives over the paper, shredding it to garbage and mud.

Ellen makes a garbled sound. "I'll leave. If it will make it better, I'll leave." I quickly hold her as the dusk moves into the room and covers us. "Don't leave. Don't leave." I feel her sturdy back shiver against my hands. She kisses my throat, and her arms tighten as we move closer. "Ah, Mary, I love you so much." As the tears threaten our eyes, the taste of salt is on our lips and tongues. We stare into ourselves, touching the place of pain, reaching past the fear, the guilt, the anger, the loneliness.

We go to our room. It is beautiful again. I am seeing it new. The sun is barely there. The colors of cream, brown, green mixing with the wood floor. The rug with its design of wild birds. The black ash basket glowing on the dresser, holding a bouquet of dried flowers bought at a vendor's stand. I remember the old woman, laughing and speaking rapidly in Polish as she wrapped the blossoms in newspaper. Ellen undresses me as I cry. My desire for her breaking through the heartbreak we share. She pulls the covers back, smoothing the white sheets, her hands repeating the gestures done at work. She guides me onto the cool material. I watch her remove the uniform of work. An aide to nurses. A healer of spirit.

She comes to me full in flesh. My hands are taken with the curves and soft roundness of her. She covers me with the beating of her heart. The rhythm steadies me. Heat is centering me. I am grounded by the peace between us. I smile at her face above me, round like a moon, her long hair loose and touching my breasts. I take her breast in my hand, bring it to my mouth, suck her as a woman—in desire, in faith. Our bodies join. Our hair braids together on the pillow. Brown, black, silver, catching the last light of the sun. We kiss, touch, move to our place of power. Her mouth, moving over my body, stopping at curves and swells of skin, kissing, removing pain. Closer, close, together, woven, my legs are heat, the center of my soul is speaking to her. I am sliding into her, her mouth is medicine, her heart is the earth, we are dancing with flying arms, I shout, I sing, I weep salty liquid, sweet and warm it coats her throat. This is my life. I love you, Ellen, I love you, Mary, I love, we love.

1891

The moon is full. The air is cold. This cold strikes at my flesh as I remove my clothes and set them on fire in the withered corn field. I cut my hair, the knife sawing through the heavy mass. I bring the sharp blade to my arms, legs, and breasts. The blood trickles like small red rivers down my body. I feel nothing. I throw the tangled webs of my hair into the flames. The smell, like a burning animal, fills my nostrils. As the fire stretches to touch the stars, the people come out to watch me—the crazy woman. The ice in the air touches me.

They caught me as I tried to board the train and search for my babies. The white men tell my husband to watch me. I am dangerous. I laugh and laugh. My husband is good only for tipping bottles and swallowing anger. He looks at me, opening his mouth and making no sound. His eyes are dead. He wanders from the cabin and looks out on the corn. He whispers our names. He calls after the children. He is a dead man.

Where have they taken the children? I ask the question of each one who travels the road past our door. The women come and we talk. We ask and ask. They say there is nothing we can do. The white man is like a ghost. He slips in and out where we cannot see. Even in our dreams he comes to take away our questions. He works magic that resists our medicine. This magic has made us weak. What is the secret about them? Why do they want our children? They sent the Blackrobes many years ago to teach us new magic. It was evil! They lied and tricked us. They spoke of gods who would forgive us if we believed as they do. They brought the rum with the cross. This god is ugly! He killed our masks. He killed our men. He sends the women screaming at the moon in terror. They want our power. They take our children to remove the inside of them. Our power. They steal our food, our sacred rattle, the stories, our names. What is left?

I am a crazy woman. I look to the fire that consumes my hair and see their faces. My daughter. My son. They still cry for me, though the sound grows fainter. The wind picks up their keening and brings it to me. The sound has bored into my brain. I begin howling. At night I dare not sleep. I fear the dreams. It is too terrible, the things that happen there. In my dream there is wind and blood moving as a stream. Red, dark blood in my dream. Rushing for our village. The blood moves faster. There are screams of wounded people. Animals are dead, thrown in the blood stream. There is nothing left. Only the air echoing nothing. Only the earth soaking up blood, spreading it in the four directions, becoming a thing there is no name for. I stand in the field watching the fire. The People watching me. We are waiting, but the answer is not clear yet. A crazy woman. That is what they call me.

1979

After taking a morning off work to see my lawyer, I come home, not caring if I call in. Not caring, for once, at the loss in pay. Not caring. My lawyer says there is nothing more we can do. I must wait. As if there has been something other than waiting. He has custody and calls the shots. We must wait and see how long it takes for him to get tired of being a mommy and a daddy. So I wait.

I open the door to Patricia's room. Ellen and I keep it dusted and cleaned in case my baby will be allowed to visit us. The yellow and blue walls feel like a mockery. I walk to the windows, begin to systematically tear down the curtains. I slowly start to rip the cloth apart. I enjoy hearing the sounds of destruction. Faster, I tear the material into strips. What won't come apart with my hands, I pull at with my teeth. Looking for more to destroy, I gather the sheets and bedspread in my arms and wildly shred them to pieces. Grunting and sweating, I am pushed by rage and the searing wound in my soul. Like a wolf, caught in a trap, gnawing at her own leg to set herself free, I begin to beat my breasts to deaden the pain inside. A noise gathers in my throat and finds the way out. I begin a scream that turns to howling, then becomes hoarse choking. I want to take my fists, my strong fists, my brown fists, and smash the world until it bleeds. Bleeds! And all the judges in their flapping robes, and the fathers who look for revenge, are ground, ground into dust and disappear with the wind.

The word *lesbian*. Lesbian. The word that makes them panic, makes them afraid, makes them destroy children. The word that dares them. Lesbian. *I am one*. Even for Patricia, even for her, *I will not cease to be!* As I kneel amid the colorful scraps, Raggedy Ann's smiling up at me, my chest gives a sigh. My heart slows to its normal speed. I feel the blood pumping outward to my veins, carrying nourishment and life. I strip the room naked. I close the door.

Thanks so much to Chrystos for the title. Thanks to Gloria Anzaldúa for encouraging the writing of this story.

BETH BRANT

BAY OF QUINTE MOHAWK

HER NAME IS HELEN

Her name is Helen.
She came from Washington State twenty years ago through broken routes
of Hollywood, California,
Gallup, New Mexico,
Las Vegas, Nevada,
ended up in Detroit, Michigan where she lives in #413
in the gut of the city.
She worked in a factory for ten years, six months, making carburetors for Cadillacs.
She loved factory work.
She made good money, took vacations to New Orleans.
"A real party town."
She wears a cowboy hat with pretty feathers.
Can't wear cowboy boots because of the arthritis
that twists her feet.
She wears beige vinyl wedgies. In the winter she pulls on
heavy socks to protect her bent toes from the slush and rain.

Helen takes pictures of herself.

Everytime she passes those Polaroid booths,
one picture for a dollar,
she closes the curtain and the camera flashes.

Reprinted by permission of Firebrand Books from Mohawk Trail *(Ithaca, NY: Firebrand Books, 1985).*

When she was laid off from the factory
she got a job in a bar, serving up shots and beer.
Instead of tips, she gets presents from her customers.
Little wooden statues of Indians in headdress.
Naked pictures of squaws with braided hair.
Feather roach clips in fuschia and chartreuse.
Everybody loves Helen.
She's such a good guy. An honest-to-god Indian.

Helen doesn't kiss.
She allows her body to be held when she's had enough
vodkas and Lite beer.
She's had lots of girlfriends.
White women who wanted to take care of her,
who liked Indians,
who think she's a tragedy.

Helen takes pictures of herself.

She has a picture on a keychain, along with a baby's shoe
and a feathered roach clip.
She wears her keys on a leather belt.
Helen sounds like a chime, moving behind the bar.

Her girlfriends took care of her.
Told her what to wear
what to say
how to act more like an Indian.
"You should be proud of your Indian heritage.
Wear more jewelry.
Go to the Indian Center."

Helen doesn't talk much.
Except when she's had enough
vodkas and Lite beer.
Then she talks about home,
about her mom,

about the boarding schools,
the foster homes,
about wanting to go back to see her people
before she dies.
Helen says she's going to die when she's fifty.

She's forty-two now.
Eight years to go.

Helen doesn't kiss.
Doesn't talk much.
Takes pictures of herself.
She touches women who are white.
She is touched by their hands.

Helen can't imagine that she is beautiful.
That her skin is warm
like redwood and fire.
That her thick black hair moves like a current.
That her large body speaks in languages stolen from her.
That her mouth is wide and full and when she smiles
people catch their breath.

"I'm a gay Indian girl.
A dumb Indian.
A fat, ugly squaw."
This is what Helen says.

She wears a t-shirt with the legend
Detroit
splashed in glitter across her large breasts.
Her breasts that white women have sucked
and molded to fit their mouths.

Helen can't imagine that there are women
who see her.
That there are women
who want to taste her breath and salt.

Who want a speech to be created between their tongues.
Who want to go deep inside her
touch places that are dark, wet,
muscle and spirit.
Who want to swell, expand two bodies into a word
of our own making.

Helen can't imagine that she is beautiful.

She doesn't kiss.
Doesn't talk much.
Takes pictures of herself so she will know she is there.

Takes pictures of herself to prove she is alive.

Helen takes pictures of herself.

CHRYSTOS
MENOMINEE

TODAY WAS A BAD DAY LIKE TB

Saw white people clap during a sacred dance
Saw young blond hippie boy with a red stone pipe
My eyes burned him up
he smiled, "This is a Sioux pipe," he said from his sportscar
"Yes," I hissed, "I'm wondering how you got it
& the name is Lakota not Sioux"
"I'll tell you," he said, all friendly & liberal as only
those who aren't angry can be
I turned away
Can't charm me
thinking of the medicine bundle opened in a glass case
with a small white card beside it
naming the rich whites who
"own" it
Maybe they have an old Indian grandma back in time
to excuse themselves
Today was a day when I wanted to beat up the man
in a backpack with a Haida design from Moe's bookstore
Listen Moe's, how many Indians do you have working there?
How much money are you sending the Haida people to use their
  raven design?
You probably have an Indian grandma too
whose name you don't know
Today was a day like TB
you cough & cough trying to get it out
all that comes up is blood & spit

Hulleah Tsinhnahjinnie.

CHRYSTOS
MENOMINEE

SAVAGE ELOQUENCE

For Aisha Masakella

Big Mountain
you old story you old
thing you fighting over nothing everything
how they work us
against one another   They mean to kill us
all   Vanishing is no joke   they mean it
We don't fit this machine they've made instead of life
We breathe spirit   softness of dirt
between our toes   No metaphors   Mountains ARE
our mothers   Stars our dead
Big Mountain we've heard your story a thousand times
We've grown up inside your slaughtered sheep   Move here move
there
die on the way   fences through our hearts
ask permission to gather eagle feathers
no sun dance   take our bundles shirts bowls
to put in dry empty buildings
walls more walls jails more jails agencies thieves rapists &
drunken refuge
from lives with nothing left
Take our children   take our hands hacked from us in death   tell
lies
to us   about us   lies written spoken lived death that comes in
disease relentless
Vanishing is no metaphor   Big Mountain you are no news   our
savage
eloquence is dust between their walls their thousand deaths

We go to funerals never quite have time
to step out of mourning   Everything we have left is in our hearts
deeply hidden   No photograph or tape recorder or drawing can touch
the mountain of our spirits
They are Still
saying they know
what is best for us
they who know nothing
their red papers decisions empty eyes laws rules stone fences time cut
apart with dots killing animals to hang their heads on walls
We cannot make sense
of this
It has nothing   everything
to do with us
Big Mountain I've met you before in Menominee County, at Wounded Knee, on the Trail of Tears, the back street bars of every broken city
I could write a list long & thick as the books they call   Indian Law
which none of us
wrote
We know you fences death laws death hunger death
This is our skin
you take from us   These were our lives   our patterns our dawns
the lines on our faces
which tell us our songs
Big Mountain you are too big you are too small you are such an old
old story

ANNE WATERS
SEMINOLE/CHOCTAW/CHICKASAW/CHEROKEE

HOMELANDS AND FAMILY

These are our stories
these are our dreams.

Through the everglades
we ran together
Osceola, wife, and child
in the swamps
we hid ourselves, our people.

These are our stories
these are our dreams.

One brave man came forward
in search of peace.
With a knife in their words
he died in jail.
They put bounty on his wife.

These are our stories
these are our dreams.

Some walked, some stayed behind
some got loose along the way.
Winter came, blankets were brought
carrying smallpox to already
starving children, women, and men.

Hulleah Tsinhnahjinnie.

These are our stories
  these are our dreams.

These happenings live in memory
  walk with us in our lives
As we study your books, your words
  the knife returns to us.
But we move on, we move on.

These are our stories
  these are our dreams.

We have run from your armies
  we have run to your cities.

We will run no more.
  We are camped at Big Mountain
And we'll move no more.

These are our stories
  these are our dreams.

We go forward together in love
  our humor carries us through.
And your words and guns are
  on our backs in your land
That will one day be returned to us.

These are our stories
  these are our dreams.

ANNE WATERS
SEMINOLE/CHOCTAW/CHICKASAW/CHEROKEE

JOURNEYS OF THE MIND

You cannot
extricate
my Indianness
my Jewishness
my Lesbianness.
You cannot
reach in and
exorcise that
pain, or joy.

You can take
me to your schools
but you cannot
take my mind
because
Indians and Jews
and Lesbians
don't forget
we don't forget
we remember—always
because we can't
forget.

You can dress me
in your clothes
cut my hair
make up my face
put heeled shoes

on my feet
and force me
to paint
a smile on
my face.
But I won't forget.
I remember.
Because Indians
and Jews and
Lesbians
don't forget.

In the first cycle
I absorb
all that is
about me.
what said
what seen
what heard
what I learn
as a small child
—someone places a
cowboy hat and gun
on my body
I pulling   I tugging
    off
  throwing to the floor
run in silence to
my mother's arms.
We never forget
this first cycle.

In the second cycle
I am taught contradictory
values—schooled in
white ways my father but
not my mother trusted—
forced to assimilate

made forgetful
placed on a path not
of my own choosing
I am dosed with
amnesia for years
and years and years.
I become the light-skinned
terror of my own dreams—
chased by everyone.
I become outside
the frame of the
picture.

The third cycle
begins with
alienated confusion
as the amnesia of
childhood breaks
I dig into my own
I crawl out of lies and
into my mother's life.
I look at her with
new eyes   new sight
and new ears that
demand she re-tell
the stories of old
because *she*
has *not* forgotten.
In the third cycle
I try to sort out
what is
and what is not
mine.

After five months
of not holding down
my food
after reclaiming

re-knowing
re-membering
I pick up the pieces.
and finding myself
I emerge
no longer a victim
of my own self-destruction.
I am a Lesbian of color
who refuses
to be
washed out.

ANNE WATERS
SEMINOLE/CHOCTAW/CHICKASAW/CHEROKEE

WEWOKA OKLAHOMA—SUMMER '85

Traveling alone
down narrow back roads
of Oklahoma Territory
camping alone for days
down dirt roads—getting lost
and back tracking.

The sign said "Cafe"
and I wanted coffee.
Sitting alone against each wall
we see but cannot talk—
cannot approach each other
in this town white people
are watching us watch each other.

Arriving at the museum
I listen to stories being told
stories I have heard
from my mother's tongue
told differently. And I have dared
to come to this place?

I stare at names in newsclippings
stand in shock at pictures
These people are my family—
my people *and* my family.
I am struck numb—hit too close
to home. I want to disappear
become invisible as I sift
through *their* files.

This museum is run by white women
who are telling lies about my family
and my people
And I want but don't know how
to read these records
while they are looking at me
suspiciously—watching—
Have I stopped passing at this moment?
What do they see with eyes on me?
I cannot do this
alone.

An older woman has been eyeing me
  She comes forward close to my body
and asks curiously "Things you have
  never seen before?"
I am froze. "Some," I say.
  I do not look at her but leave
knowing I will return.

DANIEL LITTLE HAWK

LAKOTA/SOUTHERN CHEYENNE/AZTEC

UNDERSTANDING GRANDFATHER

"Grandfather, you look so sad. Are you afraid of dying?"

"This is a good day to die, my son. Nothing lasts but the mountains and the stars. If I was the only one dying, I would be happy, but our people are also dying."

"Grandfather, you will not die. The people in the hospital here are taking good care of you. They say you will live many more years and it is foolish to say our people are dying. There are many of us and we have many things. We are happy."

"Yes, we are very happy. Our young men spend their time drinking whiskey, fighting each other, and shaming our people. Our children poke fun at those who have lived many summers and were once respected. We must live our lives on barren fenced-in land when once we were one with the land and could wander in any of the four sacred directions if we so desired. The happiness you talk of, my son, is the happiness that comes from possessing things. We are sad when we don't have the yellow metal or the green paper and happy when we do. This was not how we were meant to spend our days. The *wasicun* do not speak the truth. Their tongues are always forked. They stole our land, our ponies, our way of life and killed the buffalo and our self-respect. They have murdered our women, children, and old people. They burned our tipis, carved our sacred stones, and spat upon the *wicasa wakan* and the *winkte*. They did all of this while talking sweetly to us and promising many things and they do the same today. I do not trust them."

"The white people are good to us, Grandfather. Please don't cry."

"I feel a great sadness for I fear the death of our nation. The *wasicun* have raped Grandmother Earth and driven our four-legged and winged brothers and sisters away. How many of our people keep the ways of those who walked before them? How many know of Old Man Coyote or the Thunder Beings or White Buffalo Calf Woman? How many can even speak the tongue that was given to us by the Great Mystery? In return we have gotten many things from the *wasicun*—poverty, disease, greed, rage, drunkenness, hopelessness."

"Times have changed, Grandfather. The whites are our friends. They respect us and our beliefs."

"What you say may be true but I will not live long enough to see it. I hear the call of Owl Woman and the spirits of my mother and father. It is time for me to sing my death song. Remember the old ways, my son. When I breathe my last, remember to open the window to release my spirit to the other world. This is very important. Promise me you will do this."

"I promise, Grandfather. Is there anything else you want me to do? Grandfather? . . . Grandfather? . . . I never had the chance to . . ."

"Young man, what are you doing? You aren't allowed to open that window."

"But it was my grandfather's last wish and an important ritual for our people."

"I don't care about your superstitions. This is an air-conditioned building. We don't allow the windows open."

TALA SANNING

OGLALA SIOUX

A FREEDOM SONG

Gender, tribal origin, and treatment at the hands of Europeans who immigrated to our big island are enough to barf at.

But then: some of us are also children of the earth. And we are, therefore, among some of the most oppressed people by the Europeans and their armaggedonish religion . . . gay children of the aboriginal drum.

Being of the Oglala Sioux with almost an equal part of me Swedish, the beat of my Dakota ancestors is heavy within me. Adrenaline, physicians say, which rises with anger or an unmitigated flow of emotion.

My emotion stinks; but beyond these emotions lay the ancestral chantings of the "Freedom Song" my pale grandfather never quite understood from the lips of my Oglala grandmother who was once raped by a white settler.

I knew there was a reason my ancestors passed this along to some who still listen with their heart drums.

Oppressed people
are like caged songbirds;
It is possible to cage a songbird;
but whether free or in a cage,
the bird sings of its freedom

Freedom is its essence

Oppressed people
think and talk of freedom;

Freedom exists
wherever freedom is
thought about
talked about
sung about

Freedom is the essence of
Oppressed people

MARY TALLMOUNTAIN
KOYUKON-ATHABASCAN

....

CHARLEEN JUST NEVER CAME BACK

you know
it was private
you could hide in the tall grass
maybe that's why Charleen stayed so long
they didn't miss her right away
it was early summer
sun getting nice and hot
they said later on
when she didn't come home

Amelia's kids
were down there on the beach
all of a sudden there was
Dineega   big as a river-barge
teeth chomping grass
nobody paid attention
to those boys
they talk big
like it's nothing

well Charleen was kind of . . .
maybe just different   she . . .
thought it was fine   shirt off . . .
lying that way . . .   in the grass . . .
never scared of anything that girl
hmmmm   there was only
Dineega and her out there
Charleen just never came back

nobody could figure it out
her mom cried   some of the men
searched the river
didn't find any trace
after that the people talked
for months   kept saying
lots of bear that year
that was probably
what it was

later on Amelia saw Dineega
she ran . . .   looked over her shoulder
he was staring
jerked his head toward the woods
walked through the tall yellow grass
down there by the river
. . .   it was the way he looked
she said   he kind of . . .
grinned

(It is said in Alaska that Dineega, or male moose, is often attracted to women. If this be true, then this tale may be true.)

LAWRENCE WILLIAM O'CONNOR
WINNEBAGO

O MOTHER EARTH

Never will I plow the earth.
I would be ripping open the breast of my mother.

Never will I foul the rivers.
I would be poisoning the veins of my mother.

Never will I cut down the trees.
I would be breaking off the arms of my mother.

Never will I pollute the air.
I would be contaminating the breath of my mother.

Never will I strip mine the land.
I would be tearing off her clothes, leaving her naked.

Never will I kill the wild animals for no reason.
I would be murdering her children, my own brothers and sisters.

Never will I disrespect the earth in anyway.
Always will I walk in beauty upon the earth my mother,
Under the sky my father,
In the warmth of the sun my sister,
Through the glow of the moon my brother.

MIDNIGHT SUN

ANISHNAWABE

my ephemeral beauty
dancing into my life
after so many years,
and then leaving me
as strangely as you came

my mystic lady
of childhood dreams
has returned to haunt me,
i thought you'd left
as you said you would

yet now i see
the things i loved
before me
embodied in a lithe
young figure
of a western cree.

Hulleah Tsinhnahjinnie.

NOLA M. HADLEY

APPALACHIAN/CHEROKEE

Your body
is both the finest suede and satin.
Your scent wafts up to me,
fragrant grasses
and newly turned earth.

O my woman,
I must kneel down
and sift the rich earthness of you
between the fingers of my hand
until there is only a fine powder left.
I must know every granule of you.

I draw my face nearer
to taste the fertility between my lips
until I can find the wellspring
of that warm moistness.
The waters gently ooze and flow.

We are both quiet for a time
Listening to the springs flow . . .

Then we lift upturned faces
to the heavens
to rejoice in the whole of creation.
With this small act of love
we have planted a seed
for eternity.

BEN THE DANCER

YANKTON SIOUX

MY RUG MAKER FINE

slowly as I laid my head
upon his chest
the rain outside beckoned
for me to kiss him
we forgot the names that were called
and as I looked into his deep brown eyes
I saw the earth of his people
the earth of his blood
and the earth of his birth
looking at me

there was much to be said
on that rainy night
but talking came secondary
and not much was said
some names were meant to scald
they can break steadfast ties
then I heard the earth of his people
the earth of his blood
and the earth of his birth
telling me

he left on that rainy night
without a kiss
he went home forever
the rain beckoned at him to go
the earth of his people told me
he was going home

the earth of his blood called him
to come home
and the earth of his birth took him
from me

oh how my heart went on a dizzy flight
I will him miss
knowing this was going to sever
our hearts and leave a hole
I know the drum of his people
that called him home
I feel the pulse of his blood
that drew him there
I smell the scent of his birth
that made me let him go

I have endured the name
the scalding brand
I stand on my own feet now
the earth of my people
the earth of my blood
and the earth of my birth
told me to let you go
I listened
I know now
and we are free

CAROLE LAFAVOR

OJIBWA

Stepping softly among memories
  of the walk we walked
  on the spirit's learning journey
  I search for the image of me

Nokomis begins her thought
  as the day's light fades
  into a coyote's howl
  and the earth's edge walks away

"Gishee Ga Nong," she cries
  "travel the light of darkness
  to the world of the spirits . . .
  the center of your soul

"A soft breath from Manitou
  doesn't lurk in darkness
  but stands tall in moonlight
  to share her gifts with the People

"Indian woman loving women,
  Manitou fills your spirit
  with the mountains of your desire
  and lights your seeking path

"Manitou presses the sound of your lover
  into the voice you give it
  and at day's end Manitou
  calls you to her loving arms"

JOE DALE TATE NEVAQUAYA
COMANCHE/YUCHI

HORSESHOES

We baled hay that summer of black flesh.
Jacked off under the river's cold water,
tongue flicked the dust and dung kicked up
and moved the length of noon time shadows.

Pompous flies and horse's ass,
yellowed in the photograph of your arm tattooed.
Spigots of sweat raced themselves chariot-like
from our pores.

We could not see the wings and hides
filtering down with the cottonwoods
and locust slough, crisp and green
in their severity,
crunching like oats in our rotating teeth.

Lightning shoestringed the gray behind
our eyes, flat and hot.
Men scratched their balls with horseshoes
of dirt, and the devil in red feathers smeared
with skillet grease danced across our toes.

Evening radio static reports an icebox
robbed of its glacial memory
goes up in flatulent smoke.

Far away in the distance shoes fill
With coming rain and these tarrish words.

JANICE GOULD

MAIDU

Our lives go on, viscerally, austere, beneath our memories. You are the girl with bruised knees, summer dress spattered with blood, a lap of grief, shame, a man's sperm, something torn beneath as he pushed you down on the heap of clean laundry you carried that evening, walking home barefoot on the evening street. Myself, examining the body of a mourning dove in its shoebox, feathers like ivory and the palest blue beneath the pale browns, kneeling in the deep woods where moss and tall grasses grow and a small cross is planted. We knew how to pray and have a funeral. I know it is a place I do not want to come alone, there, or the shed, where, in the dark bicycles are stored, and old rope.

RICHARD LA FORTUNE

YUPIK ESKIMO

I have picked a bouquet for you:
  I picked the sky,
  I picked the wind,
  I picked the prairies with their waving grasses,
  I picked the woods, the rivers, brooks and lakes,
  I picked the deer, the wildcat, the birds and small animals.
  I picked the rain—I know you love the rain,
  I picked the summer stars,
  I picked the sunshine and the moonlight,
  I picked the mountains and the oceans with their mighty waters.
  I know it's a big bouquet, but open your arms wide;
    you can hold all of it and more besides.

Your mind and your love will
  let you hold all of this creation.

GAI 10th anniversary with State Sen. Milton Marks (July 1985).

Courtesy Patrick Mulvey.

Courtesy Patrick Mulvey.

Courtesy Patrick Mulvey.

PART THREE

RESOURCES

CONTACTS AND RESOURCES

American Indian Gays and Lesbians
P.O.B. 10229
Minneapolis, MN 55458-3229

Formed in 1987 as a support group and social organization.

Gay American Indians
1347 Divisadero St., #312
San Francisco, CA 94115
(415) 621–3485

GAI provides local referral services, AIDS training and education, and cultural and educational programs. Write or call for current activities.

AIDS SERVICES

GAI has been working with Indian agencies and AIDS service providers in the San Francisco Bay area to increase awareness of the Indian population and its needs. For information and local services contact:

American Indian AIDS Institute
333 Valencia St.
Suite 200
San Francisco, CA 94103
(415) 626–7639

Formed in 1988 to provide AIDS education and services for both urban and rural American Indians.

San Francisco AIDS Foundation
P.O.B. 6182
San Francisco, CA 94101
(415) 864–4376

Shanti Project
525 Howard St.
San Francisco, CA 94105
(415) 777–2273

NORTH AMERICAN TRIBES WITH BERDACHE AND ALTERNATIVE GENDER ROLES

Since 1984 over 350 sources on berdache roles in native North America have been reviewed and indexed on a computerized data base for the GAI History Project. The following list summarizes the results. These tribes have been documented as having either male or female berdaches (for example, men who did women's work or women who engaged in hunting and warfare), or other alternative gender roles involving cross-gender or same-sex behavior.

Following the name of each tribe is its traditional geographic culture area. When native terms for berdache roles have been recorded, they appear next, under the appropriate heading for male or female roles. Otherwise, a bullet indicates the type of role present. Technical transcriptions have been rendered in the nontechnical equivalents of the Smithsonian's *Handbook of North American Indians,* and the area or dialect of variants appears in parentheses.

For a complete listing of the sources used in compiling this table, the reader is referred to the "Bibliography of Berdache and Alternative Gender Roles Among North American Indians," ed. Will Roscoe, *Journal of Homosexuality* 14(3/4) [1987].

TRIBES WITH BERDACHE ROLES

TRIBE	AREA	MALE	FEMALE
1. Achumawi	California	•	•
2. Acoma	Southwest	*kokwima*	
3. Aleut	Alaska	*schopans*	
4. Apache	Southwest	•	•
5. Arapaho	Plains	*haxu'xan*	

TRIBES WITH BERDACHE ROLES (Cont'd.)

TRIBE	AREA	MALE	FEMALE
6. Arikara	Plains	•	
7. Assiniboin	Plains	*win'yan* *inkenu'ze*	•
8. Atsugewi	California	*yaawaa*	*brumaiwi*
9. Bella Bella	Northwest	•	
10. Bella Coola	Northwest	*sx'ints*	
11. Bering Strait Eskimo	Alaska		•
12. Blackfeet	Plains	*ake'skassi*	*sakwo'mapi* *akikwan*
13. Caddo	Southeast	•	
14. Cahto	California	•	
15. Carrier	Subarctic		•
16. Cheyenne	Plains	*heemaneh'*	•
17. Chickasaw	Southeast	*hoobuk* *waske*	
18. Chilula	California	•	
19. Chipewyan	Subarctic		•
20. Choctaw	Southeast	•	
21. Chugach	Alaska	*aranu'tiq*	•
22. Chumash	California	*joya*	
23. Coahuiltec	Southwest	*monaguia*	
24. Cocopa	Southwest	*elha*	*warhameh*
25. Coeur d'Alene	Columbia Plateau	*sta'mia*	
26. Costanoan	California	•	
27. Cree	Subarctic, Plains	*aayahkwew*	•
28. Creek	Southeast	•	
29. Crow	Plains	*bate*	•
30. Dakota	Plains	*wingkta* (Yankton/ Santee) *wingkte* (Teton)	*koskalaka*

TRIBES WITH BERDACHE ROLES (Cont'd.)

TRIBE	AREA	MALE	FEMALE
31. Eyak	Northwest	•	
32. Flathead	Columbia Plateau	*ma'kali, me'mi*	*ntalha*
33. Fox	Northeast	*aya'kwa*	
34. Gabrielino	California	•	
35. Gosiute	Great Basin	*tuvasa*	
36. Gros Ventres	Plains	•	
37. Haida	Northwest	•	•
38. Haisla	Northwest	•	•
39. Hare	Subarctic	•	
40. Hidatsa	Plains	*miati*	
41. Hopi	Southwest	*ho'va*	•
42. Hupa	California	•	
43. Illinois	Northeast	•	*ickoue ne koussa*
44. Ingalik	Alaska	*nok'olhanxo-delean(e)*	*chelxo-delean(e)*
45. Ipai	California	•	
46. Isleta	Southwest	*lhunide*	•
47. Kalispel	Columbia Plateau		•
48. Kansa	Plains	*minquge*	
49. Karankawa	Southwest	*monaguia*	
50. Kaska	Subarctic	•	•
51. Kawaiisu	Great Basin	•	
52. Kitanemuk	California	•	
53. Klamath	Columbia Plateau	*tw!inna'ek*	*tw!inna'ek*
54. Koniag	Alaska	*shupans*	
55. Koso	Great Basin	•	
56. Kutenai	Columbia Plateau	*kupalhke'tek*	*titqattek*
57. Kwakiutl	Northwest	•	
58. Laguna	Southwest	*kokwima*	
59. Lassik	California	•	

TRIBES WITH BERDACHE ROLES (Cont'd.)

TRIBE	AREA	MALE	FEMALE
60. Lillooet	Columbia Plateau	•	•
61. Luiseño	California	*cuut, yuliki*	
62. Maidu	California	•	
63. Mandan	Plains	*mihdeke*	
64. Maricopa	Southwest	*ilyaxai'*	*kwiraxame'*
65. Mattole	California	•	
66. Menominee	Northeast	•	
67. Miami	Northeast	*waupeengwoatar*	
68. Miwok	California	*osabu*	
69. Modoc	California	•	
70. Mojave	Southwest	*alyha*	*hwami*
71. Monache	Great Basin	*taï'yap*	
72. Naskapi	Subarctic	•	
73. Natchez	Southeast	•	
74. Navajo	Southwest	*nádleeh*	*nádleeh*
75. Nez Perce	Columbia Plateau	•	
76. Nisenan	California	*oshe'pu*	•
77. Nisqually	Northwest	•	
78. Nomlaki	California	*walusa, tahket*	
79. Nootka	Northwest	•	•
80. Northern Paiute	Great Basin	*tuva'sa*	*moroni noho*
81. Ojibwa	Subarctic, Northeast, Plains	*agokwa*	*okitcitakwe*
82. Okanagon	Columbia Plateau	•	•
83. Omaha	Plains	*minquga*	
84. Osage	Plains	*mixu'ga*	
85. Oto	Plains	*mixo'ge*	
86. Ottawa	Northeast		•
87. Papago	Southwest	*ge kuhkunaj*	•
88. Patwin	California	•	

TRIBES WITH BERDACHE ROLES (Cont'd.)

TRIBE	AREA	MALE	FEMALE
89. Pawnee	Plains	•	•
90. Pima	Southwest	*wiik'ovat, ge kuhkunaj*	•
91. Pomo	California	*das, t!um* (SE Pomo)	
92. Ponca	Plains	*mi-xuga*	
93. Potawatomi	Northeast	*m'nuhto*	•
94. Quapaw	Plains	•	
95. Quileute	Northwest	•	•
96. Quinault	Northwest	*keknatsa'-nxwixw*	*lawkxwa'-nsixw*
97. Salinan	California	*joya*	
98. San Felipe	Southwest	*kokwima*	
99. San Juan	Southwest	*kwidó*	
100. Sanpoil	Columbia Plateau	*sinlhisp-siwi'xu*	*sinta'-xlau'wam*
101. Santa Ana	Southwest	*kokwima*	
102. Santo Domingo	Southwest	*kokwima*	•
103. Sauk	Northeast	*i-coo-coo-a*	
104. Shasta	California	*gituk'uwahi*	•
105. Shoshoni	Great Basin	*tubasa*	*nuwuduka, waippu sungwe*
106. Sinkyone	California	•	
107. Siuslaw	Northwest	•	
108. Southern Paiute	Great Basin	•	
109. Spokane	Columbia Plateau	•	
110. Squamish	Northwest	•	
111. Thompson	Columbia Plateau	•	•
112. Timucua	Southeast	•	•
113. Tipai	California	*jotes*	•
114. Tlingit	Northwest	*gatxan*	•

TRIBES WITH BERDACHE ROLES (*Cont'd.*)

TRIBE	AREA	MALE	FEMALE
115. Tolowa	California	*minhushre*	
116. Tubatulabal	California	*huiy*	
117. Tutuni	Northwest	•	
118. Ute	Great Basin	*tuwasawits*	•
119. Walapai	Southwest	•	
120. Wappo	California	•	•
121. Washo	Great Basin	•	•
122. Winnebago	Northeast	*shiange*	•
123. Wintu	California	•	•
124. Wishram	Columbia Plateau	*ik!e'laskait*	
125. Wiyot	California	•	•
126. Yamasee	Southeast	•	
127. Yana	California	*law'ya*	
128. Yavapai	Southwest		•
129. Yokuts	California	*tono'cheem*, *lokowitnono* (Tulare Yokut)	
130. Yuki	California	*iwap-naip*	*musp-iwap naip*
131. Yuma	Southwest	*elxa'*	*kwe'rhame*
132. Yurok	California	*wegern*	•
133. Zuni	Southwest	*lhamana*	*katsotse*

CONTRIBUTOR NOTES

PAULA GUNN ALLEN

Paula Gunn Allen (Laguna Pueblo/Sioux) has been teaching, studying, and writing about American Indian life and thought for over fifteen years. Her poetry, essays, and fiction have appeared in such books as *Shadow Country, The Woman Who Owned the Shadows, Studies in American Indian Literature,* and *The Sacred Hoop: Recovering the Feminine in American Indian Traditions.* She is currently Professor of Native American Studies at the University of California at Berkeley.

BEN THE DANCER

Ben the Dancer (Yankton Sioux) grew up on the Rosebud reservation in South Dakota. Since the age of sixteen, he has had two major interests: dancing and preserving Indian culture. He currently studies dance at the University of Kansas.

BETH BRANT

Beth Brant is a Bay of Quinte Mohawk from Theyindenaga reserve in Canada. After raising three daughters, she began writing following a trip through the Mohawk Valley, where a bald eagle flew in front of her car, sat in a tree, and instructed her to write. She edited *A Gathering of Spirit*, an anthology of writings by native women, and has published her own stories and poetry in *Mohawk Trail.*

CHRYSTOS

Chrytos was born in San Francisco of a Menominee father and a Lithuanian/Alsace-Lorraine mother. A lesbian since the age of seventeen, she has watched the rise of our increasing freedom with relief and joy. She is active with Women for Big Mountain in Seattle. A collection of her work appears in *Not Vanishing*.

JANICE GOULD

Janice Gould (Maidu) was raised in the San Francisco Bay Area. She graduated from the University of California in 1983 and is completing a thesis on Native American women poets for an M.A. in English.

NOLA M. HADLEY

Nola Hadley was born in southern Ohio of Metis heritage (Irish, and German Appalachian and Cherokee). She began writing when she moved to California in 1973. She is completing a doctoral degree, focusing on Appalachian women's history, and is Assistant Editor for the *Children's Advocate* newspaper.

MAURICE KENNY

Maurice Kenny (Mohawk) is recognized as a leading American Indian poet. He lives alternately at the Akwesasne Mohawk reservation and in Brooklyn, New York. Recent works include *Between Two Rivers: Selected Poems, Is Summer This Bear, Blackrobe,* and *The Mama Poems.*

RICHARD LA FORTUNE

Richard La Fortune is half Yupik Eskimo, born in Bethel, Alaska. He currently lives in Minnesota and is employed at a private school for mentally retarded persons. He is pursuing music studies and traditional healing and spiritual ways.

CAROLE LA FAVOR

Carole La Favor (Ojibwa) works as a registered nurse at an inpatient gay/lesbian chemical dependency treatment center. She lives in the spirit of the traditional way with her daughter in Minneapolis.

JOE LAWRENCE LEMBO

Joe Lawrence Lembo (Cherokee) is an artist living in San Francisco. During his travels in the Southwest, he became inspired by the Hopi Indians, producing works that have been shown in a variety of local exhibitions.

DANIEL LITTLE HAWK

Daniel Little Hawk (Lakota/Southern Cheyenne/Aztec) is from Minnesota and currently lives in the Twin Cities. He received a degree in psychology and biology from the University of Minnesota in 1986 and currently works with psychiatric patients in a hospital. He is active in Guatemalan solidarity and a local ministry to people with AIDS.

JOE DALE TATE NEVAQUAYA

Joe Dale Tate Nevaquaya (Comanche/Yuchi) was raised by his Yuchi grandmother in Oklahoma and began writing at an early age. He attended the Institute of American Indian Arts in Santa Fe, and his work has appeared in such publications as *The Clouds Threw This Light*, *Contact II*, and *Akwekon.*

LAWRENCE WILLIAM O'CONNOR

Lawrence William O'Connor (Winnebago) lives in Chicago. "The great pride I have in my heritage has helped to instill in me that same sense of pride in being a gay person." His poem is dedicated to the Chicago American Indian community.

DEBRA S. O'GARA

Debra O'Gara is an Alaskan Tlingit Indian, active in Seattle's lesbian and gay community for several years. A University of Washington graduate and currently a law school student, she is a member of Radical Women, a national socialist feminist organization, and is active in defending Northwest Indian fishing rights.

M. OWLFEATHER

Owlfeather (Shoshone-Metis/Cree) has been actively preserving and perpetuating the traditions and customs of his people for the past twenty years. He is a published author, a poet, and a collector of Indian art. A professional in the field of law, he is currently restoring a log cabin built in the 1870s with his brother/friend, a working cowboy from Wyoming.

ERNA PAHE

Erna Pahe (Navajo) is a single mother of two. She has been active in the gay American Indian community of San Francisco since 1980.

KIERAN PRATHER

Kieran Prather (non-Indian) has a master's degree in linguistics and literature from the University of Southern California. He lives in Los Angeles where he is a freelance writer. He has been close friends with "Jerry" for several years.

WILL ROSCOE

Will Roscoe is a historian and community organizer. A non-Indian member of GAI, he has served as coordinator of the History Project since its founding in 1984. His own research has been widely presented in a slide-lecture program, "The Zuni Man-Woman: A Traditional Gay Role."

TALA SANNING

Tala Sanning was born in Los Angeles of mixed Sioux/Northern European ancestry. He currently lives in the California desert, where he is involved in conservation and gay rights issues. A free-lance writer, his articles have appeared in a variety of newspapers and magazines.

DANIEL-HARRY STEWARD

Daniel-Harry Steward (Wintu) traces the other side of his Native American ancestry back to the arrival of the first white settlers in northern California. "As a child I would sometimes hear fragments of stories. In the old days, a storyteller was considered a visionary, a special interpreter, who could describe that which is unseen, the sound never heard, and the old Gods who will always be. I am continuing that tradition of storytelling."

MIDNIGHT SUN

Midnight Sun (Anishnawbe) is a lesbian feminist who lives in Toronto. She has a degree in anthropology/women's studies and is training as a carpenter. Her work has appeared in *A Gathering of Spirit, The Clouds Threw This Light,* and *First People, First Voices.* She was co-editor for the native women's issue of *Fireweed.*

MARY TALLMOUNTAIN

Mary TallMountain (Koyukon-Athabascan) is a widely published poet and writer. A nongay friend and supporter of GAI, she has read her work at many GAI events.

HULLEAH TSINHNAHJINNIE

A photographer and graphic designer, Hulleah Tsinhnahjinnie (Navajo) has worked as a substitute teacher, white-water guide, editor, and program coordinator. She lives in Oakland, California, and her work has been shown in many local exhibits.

ANNE WATERS

Anne Waters (Seminole/Choctaw/Chickasaw/Cherokee) has studied at seven universities and taught at six. She currently teaches feminist theory and values at Purdue University in Indiana. An activist, she seeks peace, writes poetry, and loves.

SOURCES AND SUGGESTED READING

SOURCES

Allen, Paula Gunn. 1981. Lesbians in American Indian cultures. *Conditions* 7 :67–87.

Angelino, Henry, and Shedd, Charles. 1955. A note on berdache. *American Anthropologist* 57 :121–26.

Beckwourth, James P. 1931. *The life and adventures of James P. Beckwourth*, ed. T. D. Bonner. New York : Alfred A. Knopf.

Benedict, Ruth. 1959. *Patterns of culture.* Boston : Houghton Mifflin.

Berger, Thomas. 1964. *Little Big Man.* New York : Dial Press.

Blackwood, Evelyn. 1984. Sexuality and gender in certain American Indian tribes : The case of cross-gender females. *Signs : The Journal of Women in Culture and Society* 10(1) :27–42.

Blevins, Wilfrid. 1973. *Give your heart to the hawks : A tribute to the mountain men.* Los Angeles : Nash Publishing.

Blumberg, Rae Lesser. 1978. *Stratification : Socio-economic and sexual inequality.* Iowa : William Brown Co.

Boas, Franz. 1898. The mythology of the Bella Coola Indians. *Memoirs of the American Museum of Natural History* 2(2).

Bullough, Vern. 1979. *Homosexuality : A history.* New York : New American Library.

Bunker, Robert. 1956. *Other men's skies.* Bloomington : Indiana University Press.

Bunzel, Ruth L. 1972. *The Pueblo potter : A study in creative imagination in primitive art.* New York : Dover Publications.

Casagrande, Louis B., and Bourns, Phillips. 1983. *Side trips : The photography of Sumner W. Matteson 1898–1908.* Milwaukcc : Milwaukee Public Museum and the Science Museum of Minnesota.

Catlin, George. 1973*a*. *Letters and notes on the manners, customs, and* conditions of the North American Indians, vol. 1. New York: Dover Publications.

———. 1973*b*. *Letters and notes on the manners, customs, and conditions of the North American Indians*, vol. 2. New York: Dover Publications.

Coreal, François. 1722. *Voyages de François Coreal aux Index Occidentales . . .*, vol. 1. Amsterdam: J. Frederic Bernard.

Crowe, Keith J. 1974. *A history of the original peoples of Northern Canada*. Montreal: Arctic Institute of North America/McGill-Queen's University Press.

Denig, Edwin T. 1953. Of the Crow nation, ed. John C. Ewers. *Bureau of American Ethnology Bulletin* 151.

———. 1961. *Five Indian tribes of the upper Missouri*, ed. John C. Ewers. Norman: University of Oklahoma Press.

Devereux, George. 1937. Institutionalized homosexuality of the Mohave Indians. *Human Biology* 9:498–527.

DeVoto, Bernard, ed. 1953. *The Journals of Lewis and Clark*. Boston: Houghton Mifflin.

Dodge, Richard Irving. 1883. *Our wild Indians: Thirty-three years' personal experience among the Red Men of the Great West*. Hartford, CT: A.D. Worthington.

Driver, Harold. 1969. *Indians of North America*. Chicago: University of Chicago Press.

Dutton, Bertha. 1976. *The Ranchería, Ute, and Southern Paiute peoples*. Englewood Cliffs, NJ: Prentice-Hall.

Ewers, John C. 1948. Gustavus Sohon's portraits of Flathead and Pend D'Oreille Indians, 1854. *Smithsonian Miscellaneous Collections* 110(7).

Fire/Lame Deer, John and Erdoes, Richard. 1972. *Lame Deer: Seeker of visions*. New York: Simon and Schuster.

Garraghan, Gilbert H. 1938. *The Jesuits of the middle United States*, vol. 2. New York: America Press.

Gifford, Edward Winslow. 1931. The Kamia of Imperial Valley. *Bureau of American Ethnology Bulletin* 97.

Gould, Richard A. 1978. Tolowa. In *Handbook of North American Indians*, vol. 8, ed. Robert F. Heizer, pp. 128–36. Washington, DC: Smithsonian Institution.

Grinnell, George B. 1923. *The Cheyenne Indians: Their history and ways of life*, vol. 2. New Haven: Yale University Press.

Gunn, John M. 1916. *Schat-Chen: History, traditions and narratives of the Queres Indians of Laguna and Acoma*. Albuquerque, NM: Albright and Anderson.

Hammond, William A. 1887. *Sexual impotence in the male and female.* Detroit: George S. Davis.

Henry, Alexander. 1897. In *New light on the early history of the greater Northwest: The manuscript journals of Alexander Henry and of David Thompson,* vol. 1, ed. Elliott Coues. New York: Francis P. Harper.

Hill, Willard W. 1935. The status of the hermaphrodite and transvestite in Navaho culture. *American Anthropologist* 37:273–79.

———. 1938. The agricultural and hunting methods of the Navaho Indians. *Yale University Publications in Anthropology* 18.

Hoebel, E. Adamson. 1960. *The Cheyennes: Indians of the Great Plains.* New York: Holt, Rinehart and Winston.

Hurdy, John Major. 1970. *American Indian religions.* Los Angeles: Sherbourne Press.

James, George Wharton. n.d. Zuni and 2 Modern Witchcraft Trials, typescript. George Wharton James Collection, Southwest Museum, Los Angeles.

Kenny, Maurice. 1975/76. Tinselled bucks: An historical study in Indian homosexuality. *Gay Sunshine* 26/27:15–17.

Klah, Hasteen. 1942. *Navajo creation myth: The story of the emergence.* Santa Fe: Museum of Navaho Ceremonial Art, Navajo Religion Series, vol. 1.

Kroeber, Alfred L. 1940. Psychosis or social sanction. *Character and Personality* 3(3):204–15.

———. 1976. *Handbook of the Indians of California.* New York: Dover Publications.

Kurz, Rudolph F. 1937. Journal of Rudolph Friederich Kurz, ed. J.N.B. Hewitt. *Bureau of American Ethnology Bulletin* 115.

Laudonniere, Rene Goulaine de. 1904. In *The principal navigations, voyages, traffiques, and discoveries of the English nation,* vol. 9, ed. Richard Hakluyt, pp. 1–82. Glasgow: James MacLehose and Sons.

Le Moyne, Jacques. 1965. Narrative of Le Moyne. In *The new world: The first pictures of America,* ed. Stefan Lorant, pp. 33–86. New York: Duell, Sloan and Pearce.

Lewis, Oscar. 1941. The manly-hearted women among the North Peigan. *American Anthropologist* 43:173–87.

Lowie, Robert H. 1912. Social life of the Crow Indians. *Anthropological Papers of the American Museum of Natural History* 9(2).

———. 1935. *The Crow Indians.* New York: Farrar and Rinehart.

Lurie, Nancy Oestreich, ed. 1973. *Mountain Wolf Woman, sister of Crashing Thunder: The autobiography of a Winnebago Indian.* Ann Arbor: University of Michigan Press.

McIlwraith, T. F. 1948*a*. *The Bella Coola Indians*, vol. 1. Toronto: University of Toronto Press.

———. 1948*b*. *The Bella Coola Indians*, vol. 2. Toronto: University of Toronto Press.

McIntosh, Mary. 1981. The homosexual role. In *The making of the modern homosexual*, ed. Kenneth Plummer, pp. 30–44. London: Hutchinson and Co.

Manfred, Frederick F. 1954. *Lord Grizzly*. New York: McGraw-Hill.

Martin, Kay, and Voorhies, B. 1975. *Female of the species*. New York: Columbia University Press.

Mead, Margaret. 1949. *Male and female: A study of the sexes in a changing world*. New York: William Morrow.

Medicine, Beatrice. 1983. "Warrior women"—sex role alternatives for Plains Indian women. In *The hidden half*, ed. P. Albers and B. Medicine, pp. 267–80. Lanham, MD: University Press of America.

Michelson, Truman. 1925. The mythical origin of the White Buffalo Dance of the Fox Indians. *Bureau of American Ethnology Annual Report* 40:23–289.

Miller, Alfred Jacob. 1951. *The West of Alfred Jacob Miller*, ed. Marvin C. Ross. Norman: University of Oklahoma Press.

Newcomb, Franc Johnson. 1964. *Hosteen Klah: Navaho medicine man and sand painter*. Norman: University of Oklahoma Press.

O'Bryan, Aileen. 1956. The Dîné: Origin myths of the Navaho Indians. *Bureau of American Ethnology Bulletin* 163.

O'Meara, Walter. 1962. *The last portage*. Boston: Houghton Mifflin.

Owen, Mary Alicia. 1902. Folk-lore of the Musquakie Indians of North America. *Publications of the Folk-lore Society* (London) 51.

Palou, Francisco. 1913. *Life and apostolic labors of the venerable Father Junipero Serra*, trans. C. Scott Williams. Pasadena, CA: George Wharton James.

Pandey, Triloki Nath. 1972. Anthropologists at Zuni. *Proceedings of the American Philosophical Society* 116(4):321–37.

Pareja, Francisco de. 1976. In *Gay American history: Lesbians and gay men in the U.S.A.*, ed. Jonathan Katz, pp. 286–87. New York: Thomas Y. Crowell.

Parsons, Elsie Clews. 1923. Laguna genealogies. *Anthropological Papers of the American Museum of Natural History* 19(5).

Point, Nicolas. 1967. *Wilderness kingdom: Indian life in the Rocky Mountains, 1840–1847*, trans. Joseph P. Donnelly. New York: Holt, Rinehart and Winston.

Radin, Paul. 1963. *The autobiography of a Winnebago Indian.* New York: Dover Publications.

———. 1972. *The trickster: A study in American Indian mythology.* New York: Schocken.

Reichard, Gladys A. 1969. *Social life of the Navajo Indians.* New York: AMS Press.

Roscoe, Will. 1987. Bibliography of berdache and alternative gender roles among North American Indians. *Journal of Homosexuality* 14(3/4): 81–171.

———. 1988. We'wha and Klah: The American Indian berdache as artist and priest. *American Indian Quarterly* 12(2).

Rubin, Gayle. 1975. The traffic in women: Notes on the political economy of sex. In *Toward an anthropology of women*, ed. Rayna Reiter, pp. 157–210. New York: Monthly Review.

Sandoz, Mari. 1953. *Cheyenne autumn.* New York: Avon Books.

Schoolcraft, Henry R. 1834. *Narrative of an expedition through the upper Mississippi to Itasca Lake . . . in 1832.* New York: Harper and Brothers.

Schultz, James Willard. 1916. *Blackfeet tales of Glacier National Park.* Boston: Houghton Mifflin.

———. 1919. *Running Eagle: The warrior girl.* Boston: Houghton Mifflin.

Simms, S. C. 1903. Crow Indian hermaphrodites. *American Anthropologist*, n.s., 5:580–81.

Stephan, Alexander M. 1929. Hopi tales. *Journal of American Folklore* 42:1–72.

Stevenson, Matilda C. 1904. The Zuñi Indians: Their mythology, esoteric societies, and ceremonies. *Bureau of American Ethnology Annual Report* 23.

Teit, James A. 1917. Okanagon tales. *Memoirs of the American Folk-Lore Society* 11:65–97.

Torquemada, Fray Juan de. 1943. *Monarquia Indiana*, 3rd ed., vol. 2. Mexico City: Salvador Chavez Hayhoe.

Walker, James R. 1980. *Lakota belief and ritual*, ed. Raymond J. DeMallie and Elaine A. Jahner. Lincoln: University of Nebraska Press.

Wallace, William J. 1978. Hupa, Chilula, and Whilkut. In *Handbook of North American Indians*, vol. 8, ed. Robert F. Heizer, pp. 164–79. Washington, DC: Smithsonian Institution.

Ware, Eugene F. 1960. *The Indian war of 1864.* New York: St. Martin's Press.

Weeks, Jeffrey and Plummer, Kenneth. 1981. Postscript: "The Homosexual role" revisited. In *The making of the modern homosexual*, ed. Kenneth Plummer, pp. 44–49. London: Hutchinson and Co.

Whitehead, Harriet. 1981. The bow and the burden strap: A new look at institutionalized homosexuality in native North America. In *Sexual meanings: The cultural construction of gender and sexuality*, ed. Sherry B. Ortner and Harriet Whitehead, pp. 80–115. New York: Cambridge University Press.

Williams, Walter L. 1986. *The spirit and the flesh: Sexual diversity in American Indian culture*. Boston: Beacon Press.

Wilson, Edmund. 1956. *Red, black, blond and olive*. New York: Oxford University Press.

Wilson, Elinor. 1972. *Jim Beckwourth: Black mountain man and war chief of the Crows*. Norman: University of Oklahoma Press.

Young, Robert W., and Morgan, William. 1980. *The Navajo language: A grammar and colloquial dictionary*. Albuquerque: University of New Mexico Press.

SUGGESTED READING

Allen, Paula Gunn. 1986. *The sacred hoop: Recovering the feminine in American Indian traditions*. Boston: Beacon Press.

Brant, Beth. 1985. *Mohawk Trail*. Ithaca, NY: Firebrand.

Brant, Beth, .ed. 1984. *A gathering of spirit: Writing and art by North American Indian women*, 2d ed. Montpelier, VT: Sinister Wisdom.

Callender, Charles, and Kochems, Lee M. 1983. The North American berdache. *Current Anthropology* 24(4):443–70.

Cameron, Anne. 1981. *Daughters of Copper Woman*. Vancouver, BC: Press Gang.

Chrystos. 1988. *Not vanishing*. Vancouver, BC: Press Gang.

Courouve, Claude. 1982. The word "bardache." *Gay Books Bulletin* 8:18–19.

Duberman, Martin B. 1982. 1965 Native American transvestism. *New York Native*, 21 June–4 July:12, 46.

Duberman, Martin B., Eggan, Fred, and Clemmer, Richard O. 1979. Documents in Hopi Indian sexuality: Imperialism, culture, and resistance. *Radical History Review* 20:99–130.

———. 1980. Hopi Indians redux. *Radical History Review* 24:177–87.

Grahn, Judy. 1984. *Another mother tongue.* Boston: Beacon Press.

Haile, Fr. Berard. 1981. *Women versus men: A conflict of Navajo emergence.* Lincoln: University of Nebraska Press.

Hay, Henry. 1963. The Hammond report. *One Institute Quarterly* 18:6–21.

Jacobs, Sue-Ellen. 1968. Berdache: A brief overview of the literature. *Colorado Anthropologist* 1:25–40.

Katz, Jonathan. 1976. *Gay American history: Lesbians and gay men in the U.S.A.* New York: Thomas Y. Crowell.

Kenny, Maurice. 1984. *The mama poems.* Buffalo: White Pine Press.

———. 1985. *Is summer this bear.* Saranac Lake, NY: Chauncy.

———. 1986. *Between two rivers: Selected poems.* Fredonia, NY: White Pine.

———. 1986. *Blackrobe.* Saranac Lake, NY: Chauncy.

Landes, Ruth. 1968. *The Mystic Lake Sioux.* Madison: University of Wisconsin Press.

———. 1970. *The prairie Potawatomi.* Madison: University of Wisconsin Press.

Lurie, Nancy O. 1953. Winnebago berdache. *American Anthropologist* 55:708–12.

Midnight Sun. 1986. *Fireweed: Native women's issue:* 22.

Miller, Jay. 1982. People, berdaches, and left-handed bears: Human variation in native America. *Journal of Anthropological Research* 38:274–87.

Parsons, Elsie Clews. 1916. The Zuñi la'mana. *American Anthropologist* 18:521–28.

Roscoe, Will. 1987. Living the tradition: Gay American Indians. In *Gay Spirit: Myth and Meaning*, ed. Mark Thompson, pp. 69–77. New York: St. Martin's Press.

Schaeffer, Claude E. 1965. The Kutenai female berdache: Courier, guide, prophetess, and warrior. *Ethnohistory* 12(3):193–236.

Stewart, Omer C. 1960. Homosexuality among the American Indians and other native peoples of the world. *Mattachine Review* 6(1–2):9–15; 13–19.